A Call
to Action

Praise for *A Call to Action*

"*A Call to Action* is an important read for anyone who strives to understand healthcare. The book offers concrete steps for executives and citizens to take responsibility for improving quality and easing the cost of healthcare. Most importantly, Hank is a credible voice for this discussion. He is a dedicated and tough-minded business leader who has a broad global view."

> Jeffrey R. Immelt
> Chairman and CEO
> General Electric Company

"Healthcare in America is so complex that policymakers have largely ignored it. It's so expensive that businesses have often focused only on the cost of sickness, not on the value of health. It's so confusing that patients are left powerless and uncertain—when instead *they* should be in charge. Things don't have to be that way, but it will take a genuine partnership among citizens, employers, and government to make real, commonsense reform happen. Hank McKinnell deserves a lot of credit for starting the discussion."

> Mark R. Warner
> Governor of Virginia
> Chairman, National Governors Association

"Every day, American families wrestle with spiraling healthcare costs. We need more straight shooters like Hank McKinnell to focus public attention on preventive measures that save both dollars and lives. Over three decades on the frontlines of modern medicine have given Hank a unique perspective on one of our nation's greatest challenges."

> Mitt Romney
> Governor of Massachusetts

"When many people were content to wring their hands before the world's HIV pandemic, Hank stood up and committed himself and his company to action. His calls for more investment in prevention, greater individual responsibility for one's health, and deeper compassion for the poorest and sickest among us should be heard by everyone concerned with the world we'll hand over to the next generation."

> Tommy G. Thompson
> Former Secretary, U.S. Department of
> Health and Human Services

"Hank McKinnell is one of our nation's most thoughtful experts on healthcare policy. In *A Call to Action* he offers a particularly compelling and provocative perspective on this vital subject. Policymakers and lay readers alike will be grateful for its many insights."

> Kenneth I. Chenault
> Chairman and CEO
> American Express Company

"Hank McKinnell has written a compelling, comprehensive, and definitive strategy on how we can maximize individual and public health and spend our scarce resources far more wisely than we do today. Remarkably, he has combined fact-based, practical advice with his strategic analysis and has created a highly readable work for all stakeholders, including consumers."

> Michael J. Critelli
> Chairman and CEO
> Pitney Bowes Inc.

A Call to Action

Taking Back Healthcare for Future Generations

Hank McKinnell, Chairman
and CEO, Pfizer Inc

with John Kador

McGraw-Hill

New York / Chicago / San Francisco / Lisbon / London / Madrid / Mexico City
Milan / New Delhi / San Juan / Seoul / Singapore / Sydney / Toronto

The *McGraw·Hill* Companies

1 2 3 4 5 6 7 8 9 0   DOC/DOC   0 9 8 7 6 5

ISBN 0-07-144808-X

This publication is designed to provide accurate and authoritative information in regard to the subject matter covered. It is sold with the understanding that neither the author nor the publisher is engaged in rendering legal, accounting, or other professional service. If legal advice or other expert assistance is required, the services of a competent professional person should be sought.

> —*From a Declaration of Principles jointly adopted by Committee of the American Bar Association and a Committee of Publishers.*

McGraw-Hill books are available at special quantity discounts to use as premiums and sales promotions, or for use in corporate training programs. For more information, please write to the Director of Special Sales, McGraw-Hill Professional, Two Penn Plaza, New York, NY 10121-2298. Or contact your local bookstore.

   This book is printed on acid-free paper.

To Sarah,
my first grandchild, born November 2003,
and to the hopes and dreams of grandchildren everywhere.
The future they will inherit is ours to create.

CONTENTS

PREFACE

"Is our healthcare system really in crisis?"

Whether in private conversations or public appearances, this is a question I am asked quite often. It's difficult to answer because it makes a presumption I don't accept. The phrase that gives me pause is "healthcare system."

Oh, there's a crisis, all right. But no matter where in the world this question is asked, the crisis isn't in "healthcare"—it's in "sick-care."

In 1932, Mohandas Gandhi faced a similar difficulty. One of the most powerful moral voices in history, Gandhi led a campaign of nonviolent disobedience to help colonial India win independence from Britain. Shortly after being named *Time* magazine's "Man of the Year," Gandhi visited London for the first time. The entire world was curious to learn more about this diminutive man who carried so much moral authority. Gandhi was swarmed by the press wherever he went, and one reporter's hastily called-out question became a defining moment, both for him and for the nation he was trying to set free.

"What do you think of Western civilization?" yelled the reporter.

"I think it would be a good idea," replied Gandhi.

So what do I think of the healthcare system? I think it would be a good idea.

We've never had a healthcare system in America. As far as I can tell, neither has any other nation. What we've had—and continue to have—is a system focused on sickness and its diagnosis, treatment, and management. It's a system that is good at delivering procedures and interventions. It's also a system focused on containing costs, avoiding costs, and, failing all else, shifting costs to someone, anyone else.

Discussions about better health now take a back seat to arguments about cost. In the United States, a nation already spending nearly $2,000,000,000,000 a year on sick care, tens of millions of people do not have adequate access to the system. In other developed nations, rationing and price controls undermine the patient-physician relationship, degrade the quality of care, and add to the anxiety of individuals struggling with health issues. An aging population around the world clamors for relief from chronic diseases and the cumulative effects of heredity and lifestyle behaviors. Some of these we cannot as yet prevent. Others, such as smoking, we can.

The HIV pandemic is devastating the young and hollowing out whole societies in significant areas of the world. Thanks to an obsession about costs, society cannot deliver enough flu vaccine to keep our elders protected, or enough prenatal care to defend against preventable diseases in newborns. People around the world search in vain for the kinds of coordinated services—education, prevention, early intervention, health management—that can keep us all healthy while actually containing the costs that everyone says they want to manage.

Today, in healthcare we have it entirely backwards. We're like a community that builds the best fire-fighting capability in the world but stops inspecting buildings or teaching kids about fire prevention. Fighting fires is sometimes necessary, and we must be prepared to do that with the most modern technology available. But firefighters around the world will tell you that they'd rather prevent fires than fight them.

I am worried that we are going down the wrong path to effective, accessible, and inclusive healthcare systems. There is so much deeply amiss with the incentives guiding the people—both providers and patients—who drive these systems, and who ultimately entrust their lives to them.

Don't get me wrong; individuals are not to blame. There are no villains here. Our path is paved with good intentions. Unfortunately, the paving stones are interspersed with landmines that, despite the best intentions of conscientious people, persist in undercutting genuine reform.

My experience in a 30-plus-year career in healthcare suggests that the way we are defining this crisis limits the solutions. *A Call to Action* proposes a fresh way to define the crisis. This book is anchored in the facts—which might not always be appetizing or convenient, but must be respected and inform our actions. The proposals that flow from considering these facts in new ways might be seen by some as startling in their simplicity. I see them as hopeful in their possibility. After many years of healthcare reform gridlock, we need a new road map pointing the way through the fog. I hope *A Call to Action* spurs a much-needed dialogue on both the call to act and the actions themselves.

Simply put, our fixation on the costs of healthcare—instead of the costs of disease—has been a catastrophe for both the health and wealth of nations. By defining the problem strictly as the cost of healthcare, we limit the palette of solutions to those old stand-bys—rationing and cost controls. What if we reframe the debate and consider healthcare not as a cost, but rather an investment at the very heart of a process focused on health? Then other solutions suddenly appear out of the fog. And if we further consider the value of investing in coordinated healthcare with an emphasis on education, prevention, and early intervention, we see how the debate might shift. We also begin to realize that healthcare need not be a zero-sum game with winners and losers.

As for prescription medicines, surgery, and other medical interventions, of course they must be accessible and affordable when needed. People deserve no less. But they also deserve more. Health starts with individuals confident about their future—people who are determined to live healthy lives because they have something to live for. By starting with prevention and early intervention, healthcare is immediately transformed from a crisis that requires rationing and price controls to an investment that encourages the behaviors that allow societies to flourish.

That is why this book is titled *A Call to Action*. It represents my conviction that the debate on the world's healthcare systems is on the wrong track. Unless we correct our course, we will not be able to make the same promises to our children and grandchildren that our parents and grandparents delivered to us: that you will receive from us a better world than we received from our forebears. We who have benefited from this promise know it's a debt we must repay.

Yet it is impossible for us to repay a debt to the past. We can only "pay it forward" by focusing on the generations to come. The basic biomedical research that Pfizer is conducting today is designed to do just that. I am concerned that my company and other research-based pharmaceutical companies might lose the capacity to advance the science that can change the lives of our children and grandchildren for the better, just as polio vaccines and cardiovascular medicines and other therapies changed my life and yours.

I write this book aware that both my mother and father had their lives cut short by medical conditions that are now treatable or on the verge of being treatable. My father suffered from age-related macular degeneration, which made him nearly blind for the last few years of his life. We are now seeing stunning new treatments for macular degeneration. My mother suffered from an undiagnosed dementia. Maybe it was Alzheimer's disease. We still have a long way to go in understanding and treating Alzheimer's, but science now offers families a handful of promising therapies, with many more to come. I saw my parents lose a decade of their lives to diseases that weren't treatable. I don't want my children and grandchildren to go through the same experience. That's why I feel the need to act.

My parents bequeathed to me a world of health, or at least more health than they enjoyed. I am into the seventh decade of my life in good health, blessed by the fruits of medical research, and advances in public health, along with a measure of luck. At the stage of life where I am now, my mother and father had already begun their descent into illness. My commitment to my children and grandchildren, and yours, is simply stated. It is to honor the sacrifice my parents made in bequeathing better health to their children and doing my level best to do everything in my power to bequeath better health to our children.

A Call to Action distills more than three decades of experience—both joyous and painful—that has brought me a special vantage point. I offer these thoughts, plans, and calls to action to give our descendents all the benefits of healthcare that we have enjoyed—as well as advances and benefits literally beyond our ability to predict. But we cannot do so under the liabilities and constraints that today weigh down the world's healthcare systems. These systems promise healthcare but actually swindle people out of both their health and wealth. You and I, our children—indeed, our entire human family—most certainly deserve better.

ACKNOWLEDGMENTS

The pulling together of the concepts and ideas presented here has deepened my awareness of my dependence upon many individuals. The new vistas explored here would not have been possible were it not for a number of predecessors upon whose shoulders I stand, and the contributions of many teachers and colleagues. To all of them, I want to express my appreciation.

First, to two central figures in my life from the past, long gone: my parents, Henry and Lena McKinnell, who taught me that overcoming obstacles begins with the courage to dream.

This book would not have been possible for an overcommitted CEO to complete without the help of many committed people. First on that long list is my writing partner in this endeavor, John Kador. Throughout my career, I have seen time and time again the power of partnership and teamwork. Good partners can produce outcomes that would elude the partners acting individually. Teamwork always produces better results and decisions than any one person can produce. "All of us are smarter than any of us," is how I usually put it, and John proved that adage through his creative thinking and grace under pressure.

Pfizer colleagues on three continents offered my writing partner and me much encouragement. Literally hundreds of colleagues have answered questions, researched issues that I put to them, reviewed portions of the manuscript, and otherwise provided me with the benefit of their experience. To everyone who helped me with no other expectation than I would weave their experiences into the tapestry of this account, I offer my heartfelt gratitude. I wish I could acknowledge everyone who had a hand in this book.

By their extraordinary contributions to this book, some individuals I do want to mention by name.

John Santoro, my gifted speechwriter, coordinated the many elements that went into developing this book. He read early versions of the manuscript and, as always, provided the right touch when my ideas needed more clarity and accuracy. Without his leadership, this book would not have been possible. Nancy Nielsen's understanding of this book and its possibilities were in many ways deeper than my own; I appreciate her insights. Robert Mallett provided valuable feedback. Drs. Michael McGee, Jack Watters, and Konji Sebati were always ready to make house calls and answer the endless questions that I put to them. My questions about healthcare policy were happily negotiated by Paul Meyer, Richard Manning, and John Sory. Gill Samuels and Lisa Ricciardi took personal interest in the book and offered valuable feedback. Rebecca Tillet and Grant Neely read the manuscript and offered me valuable advice along the way.

I am indebted to Karen Otto, researcher extraordinaire, for fact-checking the manuscript. Jeffrey Sandman, Susan Denelsbeck, and Elizabeth Nelson provided excellent guidance and editorial assistance. If there are any errors in this book, they are truly my own.

I acknowledge Jeanne Glasser, my editor at McGraw-Hill, for her enthusiasm for the subject of this book even before she saw a manuscript. Were it not for the tight editing she insisted on, this book would be twice as long and half as readable.

Finally, my family, friends, and colleagues have my gratitude for the friendship and wisdom they have shared and the confidence they have in me.

INTRODUCTION

All of us have careers. Mine happens to be chairman and CEO of Pfizer Inc. It's a great job. It has taken me across the globe and afforded me the opportunity to meet amazing people ranging from presidents and prime ministers to Nelson Mandela and Bono. It's also allowed me to work with some of the most creative people in the world. I am proud that I play a part in developing and distributing medicines that preserve health and extend life. To me, there can be no greater satisfaction.

Much of what I report in this book is colored by my career with Pfizer, and it is not easy to separate my interests from Pfizer's. Ultimately, the company, like me, shares an interest in seeing that the healthcare system works. If the system breaks, everyone loses.

A Call to Action is my attempt to find a better path to global wellness. Much of what I have to say is aligned with Pfizer's policies on the issues. But the views and conclusions expressed in this book are mine. I take sole responsibility for them. My motivation for writing this book isn't celebrity or personal fortune; all royalties are being donated to the Academic Alliance for Healthcare in Africa, which operates a major HIV/AIDS teaching and research clinic in Uganda. In writing, I am motivated solely by the urgent need to catalyze new thinking about healthcare, and, in some small way, to bring about a better world for my children and yours.

I Don't Believe in Surprise Endings

I love a good mystery, but this book won't be one. Allow me to explain exactly how I plan to proceed.

The first phase of the book sets up its basic theme—that when our most cherished support systems are at risk, we are called to rethink our most well-accepted assumptions. Everywhere in the developed world, people are dissatisfied with the healthcare their families are receiving. The near-universal experience is that healthcare is increasingly unaffordable, fragmented, and impersonal. It is delivered at greater cost and inconvenience, burdened with more limitations than it needs to be. The first third of the book details the proposition that the current system is profoundly misfocused in three ways. It is preoccupied with the cost of healthcare, it defines the provider as the center of the system, and it regards acute interventions as its primary reason for existence.

With the basic theme established, the second third of the book speaks of the pharmaceutical industry I help lead. It is a source of considerable pain to me that the life-saving industry I represent is viewed with suspicion, cynicism, and anger. In this section, I answer some of the most pointed questions that patients are asking.

The last part of the book attempts to deliver on the implicit promise made by the title I have chosen for this book. In this section I set forward a number of calls to action that seem to me most critical if the healthcare system is to be transformed. If taken seriously, I believe these actions can save millions of lives and billions of dollars over the next generation.

Here are brief descriptions of what readers will encounter in each chapter.

Chapter 1—"A Personal Take, A Personal Stake" is a personal account of my interest in the transformation of healthcare and my credentials for writing this book. If you are concerned that a pharmaceutical company CEO is not qualified to write a book about healthcare reform, I ask you to start here.

Chapter 2 addresses a question that seems almost trivial until you try to pin it down. "What Is Health?" turns out to be a formidable question that resists easy answers. To the extent that we are not clear about what health means, our attempts to secure it will be frustrated.

Chapter 3—"Reluctant Healthcare Providers"—considers how it came to be that employers are so instrumental in the healthcare of their employees. It concludes that employee health is too important to be left to organizations that do not have the expertise for it. In fact, most organizations outsource the function rather than deal with it directly. It's not easy to admit that Pfizer manages almost every other part of the business more effectively than it does the employee health plan. The chapter concludes with a description of a new prevention-based approach to employee healthcare.

Chapter 4 begins the central part of the book, in which I answer as directly as I can many of the questions and objections that customers and patients send me. The question considered in this chapter is "Why Are Prescription Medicines So Expensive?"

Chapter 5 takes on the second most common question: "Why Does the Industry Do So Much Marketing?" That's how the question is stated, but the context is, "couldn't you save us money if you cut out the expensive TV advertisements?" It's a reasonable question, although TV advertising represents a small fraction of our marketing budget. I believe our industry needs to rethink pharmaceutical advertising, and in this chapter I call for change.

In Chapter 6, I consider the question that brings in the most impassioned calls and letters. "Why Do Americans Pay More Than Canadians for Drugs?" My explanation might surprise readers.

Chapter 7 narrows the discussion by considering why the healthcare industry hasn't seen the lowered costs, added value, and customer innovations that competition has delivered to other well-functioning industries. "Welcome Competition in Healthcare" concludes that competition in the healthcare industry is between the wrong players and over the wrong objectives. One of the culprits is the industry's obsession with zero-sum competition. I call for a transformation on the basis of value-added competition that focuses on increasing healthcare value instead of dividing it.

Chapter 8—"Health Creates Wealth: No One Left Behind"— describes my conviction that investments in health pay off in greater wealth. It more broadly argues that the healthcare system must include everyone. Neither ability to pay nor quality of health must interfere with the ability of every American to participate in the system. Universal health insurance is not merely about solving the problem of the uninsured. Inclusivity is good for everyone: insured and uninsured alike. Uninsured people in poor health cannot be said to have equal opportunities in a market economy.

Chapter 9—"Consumer-Driven Healthcare: Balancing Choice, Responsibility, and Accountability"—considers consumer-directed healthcare, a model based on the notion that the demand for healthcare service is limitless, especially when someone else is seen as paying the bill. Giving financial incentives to patients will reduce use of services of marginal value. It will also give patients an incentive to seek out lower-cost providers of care.

In Chapter 10—"The Research Imperative: The Search for Cures"— I suggest that innovation is more than the discovery of interesting new molecules. The real task of innovation is to make those discoveries "sticky"—that is to figure out how to take new ideas into widespread use. This chapter takes on the goals and challenges of healthcare innovation, of which pharmaceutical research is one expression.

Chapter 11—"Information Intensive: Reaping the Benefits of Technology"—looks at the difficult problem of incorporating patient-friendly information technology into a healthcare system that resists the accountability demanded by information systems. Information technology is not the problem, and it's not a solution. But we cannot get a handle on costs, reduce medical errors, and put individuals in control of their healthcare without embedding information systems deeply into healthcare at every level.

Opening the third phase of the book, Chapter 12—"Change Is Possible: Infectious Disease and the Struggle for Hope"—assesses the challenge of infectious disease, especially the pandemic of HIV, and suggests that hope is a reasonable response. The chapter introduces themes of social investment and describes some of the projects we have taken on in developing countries.

Chapter 13 connects the dots—"Next Steps: A Call to Action Starts Here" is the most prescriptive section of the book. Here the reader will find a list of the action items I believe will require our attention if healthcare is to be transformed. Some action items are individual; others require action on a corporate, regional, or national level. Because the change we want starts with what we ourselves are willing to do, I commit to a number of action items. I recognize that Pfizer, and the entire pharmaceutical industry, has to change. The behavior of health-care consumers has to change as well, and I end the chapter with a specific call to action around cardiovascular health that most people can begin immediately.

Chapter 14—"The Deadline for Complaints Was Yesterday"—describes my hope that healthcare transformation is not only possible; it is inevitable. Our children are depending on us. I am confident we will not let them down.

A Call
to Action

CHAPTER 1

A PERSONAL TAKE,
A PERSONAL STAKE

Before I buy a book, I want to know what expertise and biases the author brings to the table. When I consider another's point of view, my first impulse is to consider the predisposition, motivations, and professionalism of the messenger. If you do the same, I offer this chapter to help you see who I am, where I came from, and why I felt compelled to write this book. Then you can make up your own mind and determine to your own satisfaction if my message is worthy of your consideration.

Based on my mail, I anticipate the following objection. "Hank McKinnell, you are a rich white male within spitting distance of retirement. You are healthy, wealthy, and well insured. What do you understand about the healthcare needs of everyday people? Do you know anything about those who work for low wages without medical insurance? Or about senior citizens trying to navigate the healthcare system?"

"And, to boot, you're the CEO of Pfizer! This book has to be self-serving. Why should we pay the slightest bit of attention to what you have to say?"

These are logical objections, and I welcome them. One thing I've learned during my career is that a good salesperson always asks for the objection. Seasoned sales professionals understand that there are always objections and they take two forms, stated and unstated. Against stated objections, a salesperson has a chance. Unstated objections will kill the deal every time. If there's any objection to my credentials, or understanding of the issues, I prefer that we be up-front about it.

Before I delve deeper into my views on health and healthcare, let me describe how my views have been shaped.

Pacific Overtures

I'm the son of a seafaring family. I was born on the west coast of British Columbia, on the shores of the Pacific Ocean, on February 23, 1943. When I was growing up in Vancouver, British Columbia, my father was a sea captain. He owned numerous small ships over the years that hauled freight along the coast from Oregon to Alaska. My father was a hands-on kind of guy. Even though he owned more than one ship at times, and enjoyed a measure of prosperity and success, my father even late into his life always captained one ship himself. By the time I was 15, I was an experienced deckhand. By 17, I was a first mate and six months away from my captain's ticket. I assumed I would become, like my dad, a ship's captain.

I'm proud to be named after my father. Henry A. McKinnell grew up on an island off the coast of British Columbia. Even though his father, my grandfather, was trained in medicine in the 1890s, my father's career choices on the island were limited to farming, logging, or shipping. I suspect he chose the sea because it offered the best chance of getting off the island.

What I remember most about my dad is how often he was away at sea. Nonetheless, he taught me many lessons, especially in his approach to his work. He was a true professional, and crews wanted to sign on with him even though his policy was strict: absolutely no alcohol on board. In his half century of piloting small ships through dangerous and often foggy waters, he never had an accident. I'm an avid sailor, and to this day I won't drink alcohol when I am skippering or crewing a vessel of any kind.

The names he gave his boats provided an insight into my father's character. He named his first boat "Seven Oaks" after his mother's birthplace. His next boat was named "Loyal," and in case anyone missed the point, he named the next boat "Loyal II." In short order came "Sea Pride" and "Sea Pride II." Another boat was "BC Lady," named, no doubt, for my mother. The attributes of pride, loyalty, and trust defined my father's character.

Another lesson was his advice on borrowing something that belonged to someone else: "The best way to show thanks for something you borrow is to return it in better condition than when you borrowed it." I'm prompted to write this book because of my concern that with respect to the healthcare system our children will inherit, we are not keeping our end of the bargain. If we don't change the way we structure and consume healthcare, the system we return will not be as effective as the one we borrowed.

My mother, Lena Wagner McKinnell, was a true pioneer. She was born in Texas to a family that had emigrated from Germany. Her journey from Texas saw stops in Colorado, Montana, and ultimately the Peace River country of Alberta. This was true homesteading. For her first year in Canada she lived in a "soddie," a house made of sod. She taught me to be comfortable with frontiers.

"We don't know what's beyond the horizon," she told me, "but there's no reason to fear it." In the pioneer tradition, my mother's family moved west and then north for more open space for their cattle and wheat fields. Even though they went from land measured in acres to land measured in sections or square miles, life as a homesteader was arduous. There was no electricity. Water came from a cistern under the house. For medical care and for all other necessities, they were truly on their own.

My mother had even less formal education than my father. Eventually the search for work brought her to Vancouver for the economic opportunities on the Pacific Coast. There she met my father. On their first date, my mother told me, my father bought her a milk shake, an extravagance at the time.

Although I was content to skip college to follow my father into the shipping trade, my parents wanted me to have more education and better career opportunities. I enrolled at the University of British Columbia, where I was initially a decent student but not initially a committed one. My goal, to the extent that I had one, saw me working in some indefinite capacity in chemical engineering. I recall a lecture from one of the chemical engineering professors during orientation week. "Look at the student to your left; look at the student to your right. One of you won't be here in 12 months." I didn't realize at the time that it was me he was talking to, and I didn't realize that I was more at home in a ship's wheelhouse than in an inorganic chemistry lab. At the end of the first year, I switched to the business school.

I eventually graduated from the University of British Columbia with a bachelor of commerce degree in business, but to be honest, my studies took a backseat to my summer's other activities. I spent vacations and every week I could spare at sea. Pay was calculated on the basis of "day on-day off" or two day's pay for every day at sea. It was work I loved, and four or five days "on" would give me enough pocket money for a month.

But then family obligations prompted me to focus on my career. While still an undergraduate, I married a fellow student. The arrival of our daughter Alison sparked in me a sudden interest in earning a living to support my family. I worked harder at my studies and raised my grades. When the Stanford University Graduate School of Business offered me a $10,000 per year fellowship, I sat up and took notice. In 1965, that was more money than I could have earned doing an entry-level job in business. For the first time, I seriously considered a career in academia. As I got into the Stanford program, I found I liked business history, as well as frameworks for analysis and research methodologies. A failed engineer, I was on the path to becoming a college professor. Four years later, I received a Ph.D. in business, and several universities recruited me to join their faculty.

But I woke up one day and realized that I might be going down the wrong track. At 25, I was about to dedicate my life to teaching and doing research about business, but I had never actually worked in a business. I decided I would get some hands-on experience in management and then return to academia protected from the criticism that I had no sense of how things in the "real-world" operated.

People are sometimes surprised to learn that Pfizer offered me my first job and I turned it down. I preferred to accept the offer of a Stanford faculty member who had an international consulting assignment. The opportunity took me to Brussels, where I found I enjoyed international work. It would be 15 years before my family and I lived in the United States again.

Two years later, Pfizer approached me about an opening in its Tokyo office. This was an appealing opportunity because I had an interest in Japanese culture. When I accepted the offer, I figured I would work for Pfizer for a couple of years and then find a spot on a university business school faculty. But as time went on, I became excited about the challenge of management and leadership. All I can say is that academia has apparently survived without me. I found Pfizer's world to be a compelling draw.

After three years in Japan, Pfizer asked me if I would run its businesses in Iran and Afghanistan. At the age of 30, I became a "country manager"—leading an integrated pharmaceutical business. Granted, it was small and in a rough neighborhood, but I was responsible for all the steps that delivered medicine to doctors and patients—research, registration, medical marketing, manufacturing, sales, and distribution. My goal was to get hands-on business experience, and my assignment in Iran gave it to me in spades. I loved what I did and I seemed to be good at it. Four years later, I was vice president of Pfizer's Asian Division, living in Hong Kong.

The Intentional Tourist

There are many advantages to having a career with a global company. Executives are sometimes asked to move to different nations, and as a result come to see the world in its infinite variety. Living in another country rips the curtain off the pretense that any one society has all the answers. It also helps the traveler grasp the common threads that bind all humankind. I've seen firsthand what we all know in our hearts, whether we have traveled the world over or lived our lives in one place. Parents will do anything to create a better world for their children.

My perspective as a parent might be a little different in at least one respect. My family and I moved among three continents and made six nations our home: Canada, the United States, Belgium, Japan, Iran, and China. Each of my four children was born in a different country. This experience helped me understand the realities of vastly different healthcare systems around the world. And although the care my family received in each of these systems was excellent, it was often in spite of the systems in place to deliver it. I still marvel at how dedicated physicians, nurses, and other medical professionals do "work-arounds" in various healthcare settings so they can actually take care of patients.

Like most families, the McKinnells had a variety of mostly routine encounters with each of the healthcare systems serving us. I noted what worked, but I also saw wide variances in quality and inequalities in access. What opened my eyes most was watching the birth of my children under different healthcare systems. My four children were born in four different countries. Each provided a different healthcare experience.

As a father who wanted the best for my family, I had great interest in the healthcare systems to which I would entrust my family's care. Whenever I relocated, I studied the training and experience of the medical professionals. I analyzed the approaches to care, especially prenatal and newborn care. I inspected the facilities and explored the strategies for routine and emergency deliveries. I also researched the designs for postnatal and pediatric care.

My eldest daughter, Alison, was born in 1962 in Vancouver in a bright, modern hospital staffed by well-trained professionals. Canada's national health service covered all of the costs of birth. It was a different time then, when mothers stayed in the hospital for up to a week after delivery.

Doctors routinely extended a new mother's hospitalization for a day or two so that the family could get their homes ready. For better or for worse, those days are over. Today, cost consciousness is enforced at every level of the system.

My second daughter, Tracy, was born while I was a graduate student, courtesy of the Stanford University health plan. We were treated with warmth and professionalism by the medical professionals at the university's medical center. The costs were included in my tuition and health fees. Tracy arrived during the boom times of the mid-1960s, when the nation was serving young families, who are generally healthy and inexpensive to insure. The children born during this period are now middle-aged, have families of their own, and are making more demands on the healthcare system. Increasing life spans spurred by advances in medicine mean that it's now routine for families to include four and even five generations, complicating the care of relatives at both ends of the life cycle.

Our third daughter, Karin, was born in Belgium in 1971. Belgium, then as now, is divided into French and Flemish-speaking communities whose local leaders compete for status and political influence. Population determined political influence. For political reasons, each community wanted to increase its numbers, so each offered subsidies to encourage women to have babies. So not only did Belgium provide a quality delivery, the municipality awarded us a bonus payment for having a child. Between the low cost of the delivery and the subsidy provided by our town, we actually showed a profit on this transaction. On a more serious note, Belgium's policy of birth subsidies underscores the realization that a low birth rate (many countries in Europe actually have a negative birth rate) combined with an aging population represents a profound threat to the sustainability of healthcare systems around the world. Decreasing numbers of younger, healthier workers are supporting fast-increasing numbers of retirees who make relatively more demand on healthcare services.

Our fourth child, James, arrived while we lived in prerevolutionary Iran. He was delivered in a general hospital in Tehran that provided excellent care to those with money. The OB/GYN who attended us had been trained at Harvard. The chief nurse was the wife of one of my colleagues. Here I witnessed stark disparities of healthcare delivery up close and personal. For the privileged in Iran, world-class medical care was available. For those without status or money, healthcare was deplorable or nonexistent.

Out of these experiences I drew some lessons about structures that support doctors in the service of patients, and those that interfere with the patient-physician relationship. I saw a lot of variability among the four systems, and troubling unevenness of access and outcomes within the systems. I came away with an abiding vision of what's important and how a nation's healthcare system is intimately tied to its destiny. Simply put, a nation that does not have its healthcare priorities straight cannot long count on the vitality of its economy. Nor can it depend on the enduring support of its citizens.

As the world's richest nation, the United States is now the fault line for the challenges facing global healthcare. Healthcare in the United States is managed by a confusing welter of insurance companies, government agencies, and private corporations. Costs are high, paperwork is choking, and medical errors are rampant and too often deadly. We reward healthcare providers handsomely for complexity and redundancy, yet we penalize them financially for prevention and cost-effective care. The amount of money wasted in the United States on needless healthcare procedures might exceed $150 billion a year. Spending for administration and bureaucracy consumes 30 cents of every healthcare dollar. Liability concerns add another $150 billion to annual costs. Yet politicians insist the money doesn't exist to extend the benefits of the system to up to 40 million citizens who have neither enough money nor enough insurance.

Although America spends more per person on healthcare than any other country, the nation's healthcare system doesn't really pay for health. Instead, it pays for sickness, which means expensive interventions, procedures, and hospitalizations. The American system is not designed to reward or even measure health outcomes. If you want to know how many gall bladders were removed last year, that information is easy to obtain. But if you want to find out how much postsurgery pain patients reported or which doctors had patients with the best outcomes, good luck. America's healthcare system discourages real competition, accountability, and measurement of value.

That's not only true in America, but it's also the case in most other developed nations. People tend to get exactly what they pay for. What we pay for are procedures, and procedures are what we get.

Now, this book is critical of many things, but I do not intend for it to be critical of individuals. The issue is the system. We are all doing exactly what the system's interlocking incentives have trained us to do. For example, in the United States and most other developed nations, insurance companies pay doctors based on the number of services they provide. If they provide more services, they earn more money. Whether or not these services provide any value to the patient is not really the point. Volume becomes its own reward. Is it any surprise that people who have found the way to make the system work for them resist reforms that can emphasize value and accountability over volume?

The lives of my children and yours are diminished—sometimes markedly so—by global healthcare systems that are failing to meet the basic needs of populations around the world. Virtually every nation is challenged to meet the burgeoning healthcare needs of its citizens. Throughout the world, governments are struggling with the hard choices of access, equity, and limits of spending. Most often, the choices lead to severe rationing and general discontent with the system. Every survey I've seen shows that people are dissatisfied with the nation's healthcare priorities. Despite huge leaps in technology and far greater understanding of human health, in most developed nations, up to 70 percent of citizens believe that their healthcare system is heading in the wrong direction. Many of them believe that the system is controlled by people who have little stake in the system and who make decisions about healthcare funding from far away.

An enduring, universal lesson is that decentralization in healthcare is critical. Services should be delivered as close to the patient as possible. I'm reminded of a visit I made to a medical clinic in Bangladesh when I was leading Pfizer's Asian operations. It was so remote that we had to take an open boat to the village where the one-room clinic was located on the banks of a river. As we approached the small building, I noticed a long line of women waiting to see the doctor. Most of the women carried infants in their arms. The clinic, funded by a non-governmental organization (NGO), was modest but well attended.

Then I noticed an imposing collection of buildings across the river. The scale of the structures looked incongruous for the size of the nearby village. It was a regional hospital built some years earlier by the government of Bangladesh. I asked to visit. As my colleague and I approached the building, I thought it was abandoned. My colleague assured me that a caretaker was in residence, and after much pounding on the front gate, the sleepy caretaker appeared. He explained that the government sent a doctor to the clinic once a week. He wasn't certain when the doctor would next have hours. The caretaker did not seem overly concerned by the lack of business.

Clearly, the local villagers had little use for a solution so out of touch with their real and immediate problems. They much preferred the one-room clinic—it was local and staffed with dependable and caring professionals. As such, the villagers ratified a concept I have come to see as nearly universal. If all politics is local, all healthcare is personal. People want a relationship with their healthcare provider that is direct and caring. They will cross a river, or even an ocean, to get it. They will not be satisfied with solutions imposed from far away, or with providers who answer first to an impersonal organization.

To me, the story of the Bangladesh clinic represents an example of a high-investment government project that failed because it ignored the needs of the population it was meant to serve. That experience also helped me learn some other lessons. First, large investments of money alone won't work. Two, government can't assume the support of its citizens— it has to earn it.

The solution to affordable, accessible healthcare requires partnership by both public and private organizations, each paying close attention to the people they intend to serve. Anything else leads to failure. Here's another story that illustrates what I mean.

In many villages in Bangladesh, women walked imposing distances to traditional wells where they laboriously collected water for their families. Some well-intentioned outsiders noticed this and, without asking them, drilled deep wells closer to the center of the villages. But the benefactors were surprised and sometimes frustrated that the villagers preferred the more distant and less efficient wells.

If the benefactors had inquired, they would have learned that the women actually enjoyed each other's company at the traditional wells. Most of all, the time at the traditional well provided the women with quiet respite from the demands of rural life. There is a wisdom here we need to respect. Sometimes the value the developed world adds comes at a very steep price. For example, we now know that the water from the deep wells was contaminated with high levels of arsenic.

Given this experience, I promised myself that before attempting to solve a problem, I would first listen to the people closest to the situation. Perhaps they would not agree that the problem needed my solution.

Meanwhile, my career shifted focus. After more than a decade of working throughout Asia and Europe, in 1984 I was asked to relocate to New York to head up corporate strategic planning. I preferred to stay in the field, but I couldn't say no to Ed Pratt, Pfizer's chairman at the time. Later, after a stint as chief financial officer, I was given responsibility for Pfizer's U.S. pharmaceutical division in 1994. Two years later, I became president of worldwide pharmaceutical operations. In 2000 I became CEO. A few months later, I became only the twelfth chairman in the 155-year history of Pfizer. I was the first chairman to be born outside the United States and the first whose career started in international operations.

I'm one of thousands of employees at Pfizer. We call each other "colleagues" because we are all in this together. I encourage every colleague to maintain a healthy work-life balance. I want Pfizer people to honor the boundary between their personal lives and professional obligations. Where that line resides is an individual decision, but I believe that respecting that line is crucial. A Pfizer colleague who neglects his or her personal life for work has a misguided sense of loyalty. It's not good for the family and community, it's unsustainable on an individual level, and it's just not good business.

All this is by way of saying that even the Chairman and CEO of Pfizer has a personal life and a personal history. Even though the boundary between professional and personal for a CEO of a public company is rarely easy to define, it is from the personal side of the boundary that this book is written. *A Call to Action* is from first to last a personal statement arising out of a very personal sense that existing responses to healthcare challenges around the world are leaving too many frustrated and far too many people behind.

Why This Book Now?

Dinner at the McKinnell house had some interesting moments in the 1990s. The pharmaceutical industry was the target of scorching criticism from HIV/AIDS activists who saw us blocking the way for impoverished people who needed medicines. My children, some in high school and college by then, often sided with the critics. They listened to my logic, but I could tell they weren't convinced, and to tell you the truth, I wasn't either. Perhaps at that moment the seeds for this book started to take shape.

Historians teach us to be suspicious of "eureka" moments. In all fairness, this book is more than the result of spirited discussions with my children. A number of experiences shook me up and, in the last few years, settled mosaic-like into a pattern I needed to address. Some of these experiences go back to my first years at Pfizer; others are as recent as today's headlines. Much occurred in the corporate setting, but at least some of my thinking was shaped in more informal settings. Our duty to children is central to my conviction that healthcare transformation is necessary, and the imperative to act in new ways. This book is one measure of my response to that commitment. For those who are interested in the genesis of *A Call to Action*, I offer these insights.

The first image that comes to me is that of young children leading their blinded grandparents by the hand. It was in a dusty rural village in Iran. The elders were suffering from trachoma, a blinding disease that in the early 1970s was very difficult to treat. When Pfizer developed an antibiotic that was effective against trachoma, the memory of those children came to me and I decided that we had to act. The result of that action was the International Trachoma Initiative, and its success encouraged me. I speak more about this partnership and others in Chapter 12.

A couple of disturbing events in the 2000 time frame convinced me that Pfizer and the pharmaceutical industry had to earn our place at the table by listening more. Both events grew out of the HIV/AIDS crisis.

On March 22, 2000 our corporate headquarters building on 42nd Street in New York City was swarmed by protestors from the AIDS activist group ACT-UP. The protestors got to the executive floor, where they attempted to confront our then chairman, Bill Steere. The activists were upset at Pfizer for not sufficiently lowering the price we charged for Diflucan, our antifungal agent effective against the opportunistic infections associated with AIDS. The protest made me aware that Pfizer had a new constituency to engage with. I was not totally comfortable with Pfizer's initial response. We had an opportunity to show humility and understanding. Instead, we became more fortresslike. It seemed to me that engaging our critics rather than shutting them out was the path to a better world. Walls are important, but so are bridges.

The backdrop to all this turmoil was a court case unfolding in Johannesburg, South Africa. A consortium of 40 pharmaceutical companies had sued South African president Nelson Mandela, perhaps the most respected man on the planet. Pfizer wisely declined to be part of this consortium, but the damage to the industry was done. A lawsuit that was originally a dispute over intellectual property rights came to be seen as the drug industry preventing poor people in Africa from getting access to pharmaceuticals. I believe the memory of this misguided lawsuit is the basis for the ongoing criticism that wealthy drug companies are letting people suffer and die just to preserve their profits. The drug companies withdrew the lawsuit in April, 2001.

Dinners at the McKinnell home became more heated. My children asked me how I could justify some of the corporate behaviors they were reading about and seeing on TV. I didn't have good answers. That's when I started formulating my insight that for the pharmaceutical industry to be successful, it couldn't be perceived as being part of the problem; it needed to be part of the solution. If Pfizer wanted a seat at the table where important healthcare solutions were being hammered out, we had to earn it by acting differently, partnering differently, and communicating differently.

Out of these experiences came a number of actions. When I became chairman and CEO of Pfizer, I sought opportunities to engage with AIDS activists and others invested in the AIDS crisis. I was asked to join the Presidential Advisory Council on HIV and AIDS (PACHA), a government commission established in 1995 to provide recommendations on the U.S. government's response to the AIDS epidemic. I also attended a number of international HIV events, including the World AIDS Congresses.

Perhaps the outreach is having a positive effect. Not too long ago, AIDS activists burned the chairman of Pfizer in effigy. The entire industry was vilified as "the problem." Some of these criticisms we brought upon ourselves. But gradually the activists and the drug industry discovered that despite our very real differences, there was enough common ground for us to work together. Activists perform a service by attracting attention to needed reform. Out of this kind of respect, alliances emerge. At one time, AIDS Action, an activist group that addresses the needs of people living with HIV infection, sent protesters to disrupt my speeches. More recently, the group gave me an award, which I was delighted to accept as further evidence that all parties are learning that we're in this together.

We are sitting on a failed health system. It is a failure economically and politically, and for the sake of our children I want to find a better way. The world is in search of a cohesive vision of what we want in healthcare. In the following chapters, I will ask questions such as:

What reforms should we support?

What new responsibilities, including in our roles as consumers, are we willing to take on?

What are we prepared to sacrifice?

If we can answer these questions honestly, and work on their solutions together, then I believe we will be on the road to healthcare transformation.

CHAPTER 2

WHAT IS HEALTH?

"Dad, can you make it warmer?"

I was a young father giving his son a bath. I carefully turned up the hot water faucet on the tub.

"No, dad!" my son yelled in that tone children reserve for clueless parents. "The water's too hot. I want it warmer!"

The temperature of the bath water was uncomfortably hot and my son wanted it to be closer to the condition he knew as "warm." His instructions were perfectly logical. Yet, because I misunderstood, I only made his situation worse. Luckily, I caught my error in time, quickly cooled down the water, and he went back to ignoring me.

This story, minus the happy ending, is a perfect metaphor for why global healthcare reform continues to elude even the world's smartest and most capable professionals. It boils down to a case of how faulty assumptions combine with mixed signals to make meaningful healthcare reform much more difficult. Our failure to have clarity about what we mean by health has directly contributed to the crisis in healthcare delivery.

At the most fundamental level, most of us think we know what we mean by "health." Moreover, we believe that most people share our basic understanding, even if we can't articulate it. I believe that, to the contrary, health is a concept that resists easy definition. The meanings that we construct about health are as particular as our experiences with illness. All this means that until we come to some basic agreements about the kind of healthcare we want, we will not be satisfied with the kind of healthcare we receive.

An Elusive Concept

We all have a gut feeling for what we mean by health. Ask yourself, though, have you ever really stopped to define health? More to the point, have you ever really stopped and spelled out what you want from *your* healthcare system?

It won't do to respond, "Well, I want health, of course."

Well, I want health, too. Who doesn't favor health?

We can probably agree that we also want freedom, fairness, independence, and high ethical standards. But you and I will likely not agree on the best means to achieve these aspirations. Nor should we expect total agreement. Until we go through a process of analysis, we are not likely to be successful in making progress. Our unwillingness to answer as basic a question as "what is health?" is the trap that makes healthcare reform so difficult.

Health is a slippery concept. Like motherhood and apple pie, we know health is good and we want more of it. Beyond that, most of us tend to take our health for granted until it is threatened. It's hard to be rigorous about something when it's as much a part of us as our dreams. If we are lucky, health surrounds us like the air we breathe; we don't tend to think about it until it goes away. But if we really want our healthcare systems to give us what we want, we owe it to ourselves to define the outcome.

I say there's a better way to think about healthcare than focusing on sickness, disease, and illness. Health has for too long been defined by its absence. The heart of defining health is focusing on prevention, wellness, and well-being. When we think about a healthcare system that promotes health, rather than a system that combats its absence, we begin to see exciting new opportunities.[1]

Health Starts with a Definition

I'm convinced that one of the problems with managing our healthcare system is that we lack fundamental agreements about what health is. So let's take a look at some definitions and then I'll offer my own. I don't need universal acceptance of my definition. Rather, I hope to invite readers to examine what health really means to them, have a conversation about it, and see what common ground we can find.

In trying to tease out what we commonly mean by health, it's tempting to start with doctors because, well, isn't health the business of medicine? Unfortunately, as we will see in subsequent chapters, the current business of medicine is concerned with everything but health. Nevertheless, I plunged ahead and asked a number of my physician friends to define health. The first one I approached was taken aback.

"What is health?" the doctor repeated when I asked him that question. Here was a highly professional endocrinologist who demonstrates great skill and compassion for his patients. "Hank, I've been treating diseases for 25 years. I can tell you what disease is, but health is something I have not reflected on," he said. When I pushed him, this is what he offered:

Health is metabolic efficiency.

Here we see the downside of the specialization of medicine. If the doctor had been a podiatrist, the definition of health would no doubt have concerned the proper functioning of our feet. You're probably relieved I didn't ask a proctologist.

Unfortunately, some doctors still cling to a mechanistic definition of health. Here's what another physician-friend suggested:

Health comprises dynamic and well-preserved blood, liver and other body ecosystems, as well as having intact and functioning cell membranes that mark the boundaries between life within the cell and that which exists outside it.

It's hard to argue with that. Now, most seasoned doctors favor a more humanistic definition, and some even flirt with the spiritual dimensions of health:

Health is waking up in the morning with a deep sense of gratitude—gratitude not for any particular accomplishment, but for simply being.

As long as we're in definition mode, let's see what *Stedman's Medical Dictionary* has to say abut health[2]:

> *The state of the organism when it functions optimally without evidence of disease or abnormality.*

It's part of our common experience to define health by its absence or in terms of what it is not. But health is too important a concept for us not to insist on a positive definition. The World Health Organization (WHO) explicitly rejects a negative definition of health and reaches for something positive:

> *Health is a state of complete physical, mental and social well-being and not merely the absence of disease or infirmity.*

We can be grateful for the WHO definition of health. Conceptualizing health as a "state" of well-being allows us to consider the coordinated components—physical, mental, social—that constitute true health. Does anyone doubt, for example, that true health is affected as much by our emotional lives as by our physical well-being? One of my colleagues in France—who reminds me that in 2002 the WHO rated the French healthcare system number one in the world—has taken the liberty to extend this definition:

> *Health gives a human being the capacity to manage his or her environment physically, mentally, and socially.*

Suddenly, health is a "capacity." In the same vein, The United Health Group offers a more nuanced definition, albeit restricted to physical health.

> *Physical health is the overall condition of a living organism at a given time, the soundness of the body, freedom from disease or abnormality, and the condition of optimal well-being.*

The question before us was very much on the mind of the late Joseph Cardinal Bernardin, the head of the Archdiocese of Chicago, when he learned he had less than a year to live. Before he died of pancreatic cancer, the Cardinal decided he would accomplish two goals. First, he would speak openly about his health and his impending death to reinforce the theme that health and death are part of life and that we cannot embrace the one without the other. He also proposed to be a fearless witness to his own journey through a healthcare system and the doctors and nurses with whom he shared his last days.

Just two months before he died, he gave the keynote address to the American Medical Association's annual meeting. In his remarks on the word "health," the Cardinal noted that the words: "heal," "whole," and "holy" have common roots in the English language. "In order to truly heal the modern world," he told the doctors, "you have to provide health, and if you are going to provide health, you have to heal the whole of society—individual, family, community—and if you can do all that, that's a holy thing." In this way, Cardinal Bernardin wove together the modern themes that actualize health: health is holistic; it involves continuity between individuals, their families, and their communities. At its core it has a spiritual dimension; as a societal good, it is worthy of sacrifice.

Cardinal Bernardin's definition of health is a tough act to follow, but let me try. For me, health is about enabling people to live the lives they want. Here's the definition I propose:

> *Health is an attitude of well-being that, when nourished by a sense of personal responsibility from within, and a coordinated support system from without, enables people to live life to the fullest.*

I have a number of friends who you might think are in ill health, but they actually pass this test just fine. Some have suffered devastating injuries. Others are dealing with the after-effects of diseases that have permanently robbed them of various abilities. Some people may appear to be sick or disabled, but they tell me they are leading lives as content and productive as they had when their health was not such an issue. I believe them, for I see many labeled individuals functioning better than many of the so-called healthy folks I meet.[3]

It also seems to me that any definition of health must consider two factors quite apart from the innate health predicted by one's genetic makeup and lifestyle choices. There's private health and public health. Both depend on the time and place into which one is born. An ordinary person born today has a much better chance of living a healthy life than a person born into royalty in the Middle Ages, regardless of one's determination to make healthy choices. Before scientists understood the role germs played in diseases, most people died of infections spread by contaminated water or contact with the sick. The public health knowledge we have—and the modern water, waste treatment, refrigeration, and food-handling systems that come with it—have greatly extended life expectancy as well as its quality.

Individual health is elusive in the absence of public health. I'd like to pretend that most of the increased health in the last 150 years is due to advances in medical knowledge, especially pharmaceutical research. But it's more accurate to admit that the bulk of improved health is more a function of better nutrition and public health improvements such as better sanitation, housing, and food safety. Providing reliable supplies of clean water throughout the world will save more lives than all the pharmaceuticals put together ever will.

How about the role of personal responsibility? We all know that whatever level of health we start with, each of us has the freedom to choose more or less health. Most of us understand that our choices around diet, exercise, tobacco and alcohol exert enormous influence over our health. We acknowledge that personal health practices, such as washing hands and properly storing food, have an impact, too. Finally, we accept that our behaviors in such areas as sexuality and illegal drug use have direct and immediate bearing on our health. The challenge is to align that understanding with permanent changes in behavior. The biggest tragedy of AIDS is that the vast majority of HIV infections are totally preventable.

My definition of healthcare would be incomplete without emphasizing a coordinated system that is larger than any single individual. This system focuses on health, education, disease prevention, early diagnosis, and early intervention. If we really want to extract *optimum* value from our healthcare investments, we can do no better than to create incentives that reward prevention at least as much as intervention. If we don't, if it's back to business as usual; our choices are limited to minimizing costs by the failed strategies of rationing, price controls, and cost shifting. What's the difference? Well, we now know that the very strategies used to minimize costs actually cause costs to increase. As a result, we are all frustrated and angry. We can do better.

Health is an expanding concept and I don't think any one definition can ever pin it down. I believe our quest for health allows for many different definitions and approaches. The road to a healthcare system we can all be proud of begins with a conversation. If you don't agree with my definition of health, I'm interested in hearing yours.

From Healthcare to Health

While we were not looking, the healthcare system, which in its dazzling complexity developed a momentum of its own, became relentlessly focused on sickness.

Let's face it; even in the popular imagination healthcare has always been about disease. Listen to children talk about becoming scientists and doctors. "I want to discover a cure for cancer" or "I want to help sick people get better," are typical responses. Who has ever heard a young person say, "I want to discover a pill that will maintain healthy lipid levels" or "I want to be a doctor who keeps healthy people healthy"?

If there is a continuum between health and sickness, all the incentives of the healthcare system now respond to signals from sickness. It's when we get sick that the present system goes to work. It is sickness, not wellness, that the system measures and assails. It's in its response to disease or injury, not health, that the system finds its legitimacy. And to be fair, the modern, high-tech healthcare system often performs magnificently when it confronts disease or injury.

So far so good, but there's another side of the coin, and it's here that we are sidetracked by confusion on what is important about health. This is the side of the healthcare system that requires payment.

If we really want health, we've created a system guaranteed to bank-rupt us without giving us the health we want. Here in the United States, we have developed perhaps the highest-cost healthcare delivery system among the developed nations. We have a system that pays for procedures, not cures; interventions, not outcomes; transactions, not transformations. We penalize doctors for providing cost-effective care that actually promotes health, but we reward them for interventions regardless of outcome, redundancy, and waste. The fear of ruinous medical malpractice generates even more complexity and unnecessary duplication.

Because the United States, unique among the nations of the world, insists on dealing with healthcare providers and insurers as separate eco-nomic and social systems, we have thoroughly disconnected the link between healthcare cost and healthcare value. The result is that health-care costs are spiraling upwards and all of our frantic efforts to control spending by rationing and price controls are, paradoxically, guaranteed to increase costs even faster.

The system is overheated by its unforgiving focus on costs. Every-one wants to turn down the heat, but all our signals to "make it warmer" just put us even deeper into hot water. We need to consider what it is we mean by health before we know which way to turn the faucet. Later in the book I suggest some strategies for a system that can actually deliver health with more choices, higher quality, and more value. But we cannot do that until we have some workable agreements on what it is we mean by health.

Since I began thinking about this book, I've asked hundreds of peo-ple around the world the question that is the subject of this chapter. I've been fascinated by the variety and thoughtfulness of the responses. When asked about health for themselves, most people offer one set of answers. But when asked about the health they want for their children, the responses often take on a different tone. Suddenly, health is less about curing specific illnesses and more about avoiding illnesses in the first place. When we talk about health for our children, we approach what I believe is the truest definition of health. It is about hope. I think we should trust this attitude and integrate the values that it represents more tightly into the DNA of our healthcare systems.

Prevention is integral to any well-functioning healthcare system. A healthcare system informed by a prevention-driven definition of health will look a lot different than a healthcare system informed by a cure-driven definition. There is some reason for encouragement. The lead federal agency for protecting the health and safety of people at home and abroad has been renamed The Centers for Disease Control and Prevention in recognition of the critical role that prevention plays in improving health. Unfortunately, the healthcare systems actually operating today pay little more than lip service to prevention. Almost all the incentives encourage interventions and cures instead of education and prevention.

If we had better clarity about what we mean by health, our expectations could be stated with more precision. More emphasis on the health outcomes we wanted would lead to better metrics. Right now, we have exquisite metrics on the expense side of the system. Healthcare administrators know to the penny what a pill, x-ray, or other "input" costs. But on the output side of the system, there is a black hole. What is the value to the individual or society of a chronic disease diagnosed, a hospitalization avoided? What's the value to society of giving an individual five more years of productive work life?

Our healthcare systems suffer from a bad case of mixed signals in which every attempt to cool down overheated healthcare systems gets misinterpreted by well-meaning legislators, regulators, and healthcare administrators. Without a clear definition of health, it is no wonder that despite our best efforts, we turn the faucet the wrong way. It's time for positive change, or we'll end up throwing the patient out with the bath water.

CHAPTER 3

RELUCTANT
HEALTHCARE
PROVIDERS

I t's bad enough when workers lose their jobs. But isn't it a scandal that just when they are most vulnerable, they should also lose their health insurance? Most people will take and lose many jobs in the arc of their careers; access to health insurance should not be a condition of one or the other.

The way we link employment and health insurance is unique to the U.S. healthcare system. It is one of the dynamics that contributes to the estimated 40 million people in the United States who are without medical insurance, or, more precisely, the somewhat smaller number of Americans who are between jobs and therefore without health insurance at one point or another in a calendar year. Whichever number you select, it's a disgrace.

If we had to design a healthcare system from scratch, would we really make everyone look to their employers for health insurance? I don't think so. Employees don't rely on their employers for car insurance, fire insurance, flood insurance, life insurance, mortgage insurance, or any other kind of insurance. So how did employers get to be the provider of this one type of insurance?

The link between employer and health insurance really owes its existence to the law of unintended consequences. It explains why most privately insured Americans are insured through their employers. The story starts with government price controls: in this case, the attempt by the federal government during World War II to prevent inflation.

When World War II broke out and millions of Americans left for the battlefields in Europe and the Pacific, factories in the homeland experienced a labor shortage. We know what happens when there's a labor shortage: wages rise. So, fearful of inflation, the government imposed a wage freeze and price controls on employers.

As a result, if you were a factory owner desperate for skilled workers but could not compete for the best workers by raising salaries, what would you do? You might offer different kinds of noncash compensation that wouldn't upset the government but would differentiate your business. You might offer free lunches, employer-paid holidays, or employer-paid vacation days. You might even throw in employer-paid health insurance. And that's exactly what happened.

Before 1942, most people got along just fine without health insurance. When my mother or father got sick, they paid the pharmacy or the doctor—who often came to the home—and everyone went on their way without too much worry. If you couldn't afford it, doctors and hospitals were willing to accept their fees over time. My uncle, a dentist, was often paid in firewood during the Great Depression. The few who purchased health insurance did so in the same way they bought life and other types of insurance, on the private market.

In the next few years, companies began to offer more and more noncash benefits as incentives to recruit and retain skilled workers. The government considered these incentives small change. It even encouraged the practice by treating employer-paid health insurance as a deductible business expense. Nor did employees have to declare these benefits as income. Government regulation cemented these benefits in place and, though the incentives were modest in dollar terms (health insurance was originally called a "fringe benefit"), everyone seemed to be better off.

Fifty years later, we can see what a bad bargain this turned out to be. While we weren't thinking about it, employers suddenly found themselves in the role of third-party payers, inserted as intermediaries between patients—the first party—and doctors—the second party. It is not a comfortable role for employers. More fundamentally, the arrangement trained employees to regard healthcare as "free," something they passively received, an entitlement at someone else's expense.

Eventually World War II ended, wage controls ended, but employer-paid health insurance is still with us. In due course the government itself got into the business of providing healthcare, and now we think it a scandal that not everyone has healthcare paid for by third parties. The government has its fingerprints all over this situation. Price controls catalyzed the present healthcare mess, and tax policies perpetuate it.

It will not be easy to reform this third-party payment system. For the first party, having the third party pay the doctor's bills seems to be an entirely satisfactory arrangement. A system that robs Peter to pay Paul can be counted on to have the enduring gratitude of Paul.

Toward a Level Playing Field

From a public policy perspective, it's just not fair that a Pfizer employee gets lower-cost health insurance because the premiums the company pays are tax deductible as a business expense and the premiums charged to the employee are paid for with before-tax dollars. But if that person is a self-employed contractor to Pfizer doing the same job, he or she must pay for health insurance with after-tax dollars. Adding insult to injury, the self-employed contractor does not benefit from the discounts Pfizer negotiates on behalf of its traditional employees.

We live in a world where workers change jobs much more than in the past. People in the 1940s never imagined a world where unemployment and career disruption were so common and the loss of health insurance so devastating. In those days, employment was much more stable and many people spent their entire careers with one employer. Healthcare costs were affordable. Hospitalization, and the potential bankruptcy it could bring, was the chief fear.

If employers had thought about the situation systematically, they would have rejected the idea of volunteering as third parties to pay for employee healthcare. Economists would have cautioned that under such a system healthcare costs would quickly and uncontrollably skyrocket, which is exactly what we have seen. A fundamental law of economics is that when the price of anything declines, people demand more of it.

Healthcare needs are infinite. Life is such that we can always use more healthcare. In the course of a day, we are always aware of ailments, minor and not so minor, imagined and actual, to which we can respond differently. We can ignore some ailments and hope they go away. We can treat them with over-the-counter medications. We can phone our doctor for an appointment. We can make our way to the emergency room. We can call an ambulance.

Each one of these responses has a cost. And when the cost is paid by money out of our own pockets, we sort these things out accordingly. But when someone else is paying, then we have little or no incentive to discriminate the trivial from the urgent, the reasonable from the extravagant. Without price consciousness on the part of patients, doctors have no incentive to keep costs down or to innovate. No one has any real sense of ownership in the system. The entire healthcare system is hijacked by the pretense that someone else is paying for it.

Which brings us to the question of who actually pays for healthcare. I can tell you that Pfizer currently spends about $315 million on healthcare for its employees and their family members in the United States. But it would be a mistake to suggest that Pfizer is *actually* paying for anything.

Whether the payment for a healthcare invoice comes directly from the patient or indirectly through a government agency, employer, insurance company, or other third-party payer, the reality is that the bill is paid by workers creating products and services that other people value. So whether the invoice marked "payment due" is for a procedure that benefits us or benefits someone else, the invoice is ultimately presented to those of us who are employed. It is a pleasant fiction to think that someone else, whether employers or governments, relieves us of that obligation.

Moreover, it is a huge disservice to the employee-employer relationship to believe that enlightened employers "give away" health insurance. Although Pfizer writes the check for health insurance, it does not actually bear the burden of the payments. The real costs are borne by those who earn incomes, whether they work directly for us, or whether they use the proceeds from their work to invest in Pfizer. From the first penny to last, workers bear the costs of their healthcare by whatever mechanism it is provided.

Like virtually all companies, Pfizer compensates its employees using a combination of cash and noncash benefits. Health insurance has evolved to be perhaps the most important noncash benefit, which is not surprising as health is the most important noncash attribute. I'm proud of the healthcare package that Pfizer can offer employees and their loved ones. We need to be able to offer the most robust healthcare plans if we want to attract the most talented team members. But not for a moment do I want our employees to think that we are giving anything away. Employees earn every penny of their health insurance just as they earn every penny of their salaries. As long as we're on the subject of employee health plans, though, I think Pfizer can do a better job of managing ours and aligning it to the values of prevention and personal responsibility. I offer a call to action about employee health care in Chapter 13.

A cleaner way to think about health insurance is not as something that Pfizer "gives away" but as something that Pfizer "sells" to its employees. The sale involves two parts, the first relatively transparent, the second decidedly opaque. Suppose you want to work for Pfizer and we want to hire you to do a job that our customers have signaled they want us to do. Economic value is created in that transaction, and the first step is the relatively transparent process of establishing your contribution to that value. We have a fair and reasonable process for determining how Pfizer values your skills and what benefits you can provide our customers as an employee.

Whatever that value is, it won't be entirely reflected in the figure printed after the "Pay to the order of" on your paycheck. That's because in part two of the deal, Pfizer takes some of the value that you create and makes you buy health insurance with it. We think it is a good deal for you because Pfizer's size and tax advantage gives us the ability to negotiate better health insurance rates on your behalf than you could get as an individual. But who knows? Maybe you could negotiate a better rate. Or perhaps you are covered by the policy of a spouse or domestic partner, in which case you could opt out of Pfizer's healthcare plan. In any case, there's no easy way to compare.

The more money that a company pays for employee health insurance, the less it can provide the employee in wages. Cash and noncash compensation come out of the same pot. From the employer's perspective, health insurance is part of the cost of labor, and those costs are borne by workers. The workers can be in the direct employ of a company. Or we can take it one step further on the value chain. We can think of the workers as the consumers (customers) of a company's products or services who transferred to the company a part of the value they created elsewhere. In the end, there's always someone working, sweating, planting, making, building, inventing, and risking. The employer might act as an intermediary, but free lunches don't exist.

Someone is always stuck with the bill. My preference is that the bill be presented to the one who dines.

Managing Care Is More than Managing Costs

Managed care is not about managing care, but managing costs. It doesn't even rise to the level of managing costs, but merely shifting them. Managed care is akin to squeezing a balloon at one point, only to distort it at some other point where it is someone else's problem.

Managed care is a monster that feeds on itself. Under the pressures of managed care, healthcare providers do things that undermine the long-term interests of the system. One of my colleagues in Manchester, England, told me the following story about how attempts to control costs backfired and actually increased overall spending. My colleague needed a sophisticated diagnostic test. To control costs, the local arm of the British National Health Service, called the Greater Manchester Strategic Health Authority, imposed limits on such tests. Waits up to three years are routine for outpatients covered by the Authority. But because hospitalized patients can "jump the queue," my colleague's physician decided to admit him to a Manchester Hospital. Was my colleague sick? No, he just needed a test. As a hospital patient, though, he went to the head of the line for the needed test. The result? Hundreds of expensive hospital beds are occupied by people who need nothing more than a diagnostic test. A report by the Greater Manchester Health Service Authority subsequently determined that up to a third of patients do not need to be there.[1] Whatever savings the system gained by limiting access to tests were offset by dramatically increased costs elsewhere.

How Pfizer Approaches Employee Healthcare

American employers have essentially abdicated their own management responsibility for health benefits. Employers have made a lot of fundamental mistakes. We buy healthcare services as a commodity, by and large ignoring the issues of quality and ignoring the issues of value. We insist on signing up for the health plan that gives us the best deal and then kind of holding our hands over our eyes and hoping that things work out.

Let me speak personally to this point because I have been as guilty as any other executive. Pfizer manages almost every other part of the business more effectively than it does the employee health plan. Employee healthcare is not an area where we have a lot of experience, and we naturally outsourced it to experts. Beyond ensuring that our employee health plan is competitive with what other leading companies offer, we haven't thought about it too much. The result is that our health plan looks pretty much like everyone else's health plan. I remember it was easy to feel that I couldn't do anything about it. If we did purchasing or IT or anything else that way, we'd be in a lot of trouble.

I thought about something one of my mentors once told me. "You are being paid to lead, so lead," my predecessor Chairman and CEO Ed Pratt said. "If you are content to do things this year the same way you did last year, what are we paying you for?" I took this message to heart. So in the last year I have started challenging conventional thinking in the employee health area. I should have started this process 10 years earlier because it seems to me so crucial that we practice what we preach. My goal is to have an employee health benefit plan and service function aligned with the broad themes of prevention and personal responsibility. Such a plan would have a number of important goals and would align our practices with the view expressed in this book.

It would, first, increase emphasis on prevention and personal autonomy to drive measurable health improvements, reduce disparities in care, and improve quality at every level. I want our employees to have more access to information, to help them better manage their diseases and conditions, and to embrace new technologies to improve patient record sharing and reporting. We have a point of view that the effective use of pharmaceuticals and a focus on prevention and wellness over treatment pays dividends. My goal is to demonstrate that organizations don't have to settle for being passive intermediaries that employees have to negotiate, but can be active partners in their ongoing wellness.

I underestimated the resistance to change and the opposition I faced from the stewards of employee benefits. I was tinkering with something that wasn't exactly broken and had been far outside the scrutiny of most CEOs. The professionals who managed this function had their organization, their consultants, they knew how to do this, and they resisted my attempts to shake up the system. I really had to threaten to take it away from them before we could get some change. The experience taught me that there is something about healthcare that is probably more resistant to change than other areas.

Here's an example of what we're up against. Even before I started this latest transformation, we were moving toward prevention-oriented programs and services. One of them is the Health Management Program, a coordinated service designed to enhance health through prevention, education, and early detection of diseases or conditions. One of the components of this service is an initial health assessment. This is a paper or Web-based questionnaire that employees can take at their convenience in the privacy of their offices or homes. A second health assessment is scheduled for six months after the first. To encourage employees to participate in this program, we provide a $100 annual credit toward their medical coverage contributions.

How does that sound to you? One hundred dollars just for filling out a health assessment? After a year of reminders and notices, what percent of Pfizer employees do you think took advantage of the program and claimed the credit? Before you answer, I can tell you that the program is administered by an independent organization. And, yes, I took the time to complete the Health Management assessment. It required about 20 minutes. What would you have done? In fact, about 30 percent of eligible Pfizer colleagues completed the assessment.

I got the predictable responses. People were meaning to get to it but were too busy. They just never found the right time. They were enrolled in other prevention programs. I accepted all these explanations at face value, but I suspect something more subtle was going on. We have been trained by a deeply dysfunctional medical system to fear that our personal medical information will be used against us. Unfortunately, this fear is not without some basis. People rightly fear being labeled or denied insurance for some medical condition that is revealed by assessments such as this. Another factor, perhaps, is the familiar human tendency for some of us to prefer denial to confronting hard facts. Some of us prefer not to know the truth because otherwise we would have to take difficult actions. It struck me that when the context is healthcare, there is no such thing as making a minor change.

It might not be easy, but I think the effort is worth making because a prevention-based approach to employee healthcare will produce savings for the company many times over what we spend in incentives. These savings will accrue through better health, and therefore lower healthcare costs. And that doesn't even take into account the savings we get from more productive employees and reduced "presenteeism"—the problem of workers being on the job but, because of illness or other medical conditions, not really functioning. As much as 60 percent of the total cost of worker illness stems from "on-the-job productivity losses"—exceeding what companies spend on medical and disability benefits and sick days. The biggest productivity drains, according to a study by Cornell University researchers, are relatively benign ailments such as headaches, allergies, arthritis, and strep throat.[2]

Employees sometimes believe that they are demonstrating dedication to their jobs by coming into work when they are sick. I think that employees who are sick should focus on getting better. They demonstrate real dedication to the job by getting screened and taking steps to prevent sickness. Employees may show up to work with strep throat, for example, but with the pain and coughing they are not very productive—and they put other employees at risk.

Presenteeism-related declines in productivity can be advantageously offset by relatively small investments in screening, prevention, treatment, and education. Education in this context works hand-in-glove with prevention. The reason we take strep throat seriously is not just to alleviate the symptoms of a sore throat, but to prevent rheumatic heart disease, a serious complication of streptococcal (strep) throat infection. That is why doctors advise people to continue taking the prescribed antibiotics for the full 10 days even when their throat feels just fine after three. While the symptoms of sore throat may be gone, the heart is still at risk.

In the United States, the Pfizer colleague health plan touches 40,000 employees and an additional 60,000 dependents. The medical plan expenditures for 2004 are about $315 million. If you do the math, that means we spend about $7850 per employee for healthcare benefits. This is just above the industry average of $7703 per employee. The program redesign I initiated was not primarily about saving money, but I am worried about the sharp year-to-year rise in healthcare costs. Our healthcare spending, like all our costs, is reflected in the price of our products. That's true for every organization that offers a product or service. According to General Motors, its employee and retiree healthcare costs on a per-vehicle basis are about $1400 for every car or truck it builds. That's more than General Motors spends for steel. We all need to find ways to keep healthcare costs affordable.[3]

From Machine-Age Healthcare

The world is locked in a nineteenth-century model of healthcare finance inspired in 1882 by German Chancellor Otto von Bismarck. The Medicare and employer-provided insurance systems in the United States, as well as in many other developed nations, are all heirs of the system that Bismarck founded. While Bismarck's public safety net program was quite revolutionary for its time, its inflexible, employer-based structure has outlived its usefulness. We need a more coordinated approach that is consumer-driven and rooted in individual autonomy and choice.

In one respect, healthcare today is no different from healthcare at the time of Hippocrates. If you ask who pays for healthcare, there can be but one answer: the productive members of society pay for healthcare. It is by the sweat of our brows, by workers creating more than they consume, that societies create the possibilities for specialization of labor, for healthcare providers, and the means to pay for them. In modern societies, employed people bear the cost of healthcare for us, our families, and those in our communities who are unable to pay the bill.

I can't resist ending this chapter without recounting my favorite Bismarck story because it's a reminder that political leaders then, as now, are always humbled by the realities of germs and public health.

The story concerns Bismarck and a renowned German doctor and biologist named Rudolf Ludwig Karl Virchow, who is credited as the first physician to recognize leukemia. When Dr. Virchow criticized Bismarck's policies, Bismarck challenged the scientist to a duel. Virchow replied, "As I am the challenged party, I have the choice of weapons, and here they are." With that, Virchow held up two large sausages that looked exactly alike. "One of these is infected with deadly germs; the other is perfectly safe," he said. "Let his Excellency have the honor to select the sausage of his choice, and eat it. I will eat the other." Bismarck, the Iron Chancellor, measured the alternatives and, deciding he didn't like the odds, withdrew his challenge.

Perhaps it is from this incident that Bismarck got the inspiration for the quotation for which he is most remembered. The Iron Chancellor is celebrated for observing a truism that those of us invested in reforming the healthcare system through the legal and political process would do well to remember. "Those who love the law and sausage should watch neither being made."

Chapter 4

WHY ARE PRESCRIPTION MEDICINES SO EXPENSIVE?

Every few days, I take some time to review letters and emails addressed to the chairman and CEO of Pfizer. I read them all and make sure that each one gets a response, either from me personally or from a colleague who is better informed about the particular issue raised by the letter writer. For example, some people ask me questions about the clinical specifics of particular medicines. In these cases, I ask the appropriate medical director to respond. Other mail concerns business or pharmaceutical industry issues. While a number of the letters are critical, most of them are also thought-provoking. I try to respond personally to as many of these letters as I can.

Based on the mail I have received in the past year or so, there are three questions that are asked more than others:

- Why are prescription drugs so expensive?
- If the drug companies simply stopped marketing so much and lowered the prices of medicines, wouldn't everyone be better off?
- Why do Americans pay more than Canadians for drugs?

Let me try to answer the first of these three questions in this chapter. The second and third questions are the subjects of the next two chapters.

Consumers in the United States are rightly upset when they have to dig deeper into their pockets than consumers elsewhere who are buying the identical prescription medicines. They see the rising costs of medicines and the rising costs of healthcare and are concerned that the first determines the second. They see all the direct-to-consumer advertising by the pharmaceutical companies and wonder if prices would come down if the industry did less of it. And given that profits earned by the pharmaceutical industry appear higher than those of other industries, they might be tempted to conclude that the world would be better served if the industry cut back on its profits and marketing expenses and simply made its medicines cheaper.

Let me start this discussion by saying that I wish I could lower pharmaceutical prices across the board. As a business person, it upsets me when the customers we serve—and who ask for our products by name—find it a hardship to pay for these products. From a business perspective, that's a significant failure, and it explains much about why the reputation of the pharmaceutical industry is so low.

I know that costs for prescription medicines can be devastating, especially for those without adequate medical insurance. We acknowledge our responsibility to help make our products more affordable to people with limited incomes. This is a very specific "call to action." Readers are entitled to know how we responded.

Twenty years ago, Pfizer launched "Sharing the Care," which made our products available for free, through community health care clinics, to people on limited incomes. In 2002, we went a step further, introducing the Pfizer Living Share Card, which provided access to our medicines essentially free of charge for low-income seniors. There's a $15-a-month prescription fee that goes to the pharmacist.

In 2004, the United States extended a pharmaceutical drug benefit to all seniors on Medicare, so we switched our focus to others who are poor and uninsured. Because the uninsured don't have access to managed care discounts, many poor or working-class people actually pay the highest prices in America for medicines and other healthcare services. That's not right. So to the poorest families, we give away our medicines for free. For everyone else who is uninsured, regardless of age or income, we provide the same levels of discounts we give to major customers, like managed care organizations and HMOs. To many working-class families, we charge only a dispensing fee, which goes to the pharmacist.

We group all of our access programs under an umbrella called "Pfizer Helpful Answers." Discounts range up to 50 percent. And for those families earning less than $31,000 a year, virtually all Pfizer medicines, including Viagra, are available free of charge.[1]

Almost every pharmaceutical company recognizes its responsibility to make their products affordable to uninsured people. Pfizer's Helpful Answers joins dozens of patient assistance programs that together offer patients access to thousands of prescription medicines at discount prices. These companies have joined Pfizer in pledging that no patients in need of their medicines will go without them because they cannot afford them. Medicines available through the programs include many of the newest and most innovative brand-name treatments available, including medicines that treat cancer, high cholesterol, diabetes, high blood pressure, stroke, depression, schizophrenia, and Alzheimer's.

While these programs can be real lifesavers, the reality is that the application process and eligibility requirements vary for each company and program. For patients who want access to multiple medicines, the barriers to enrolling in individual patient assistance programs can be daunting. That's why the Pharmaceutical Research and Manufacturers of America (PhRMA), the trade association representing the country's leading pharmaceutical research and biotechnology companies, designed a comprehensive one-stop link to thousands of medicines offered through hundreds of patient assistance programs sponsored by member companies, nonmember companies, and government and local organizations.[2]

The need for these discount programs underscores the twin difficulties of lack of access to prescription drug insurance coverage and the high prices of many prescription drugs for people of modest means. Perceptions are everything, and in the ruthless cost-cutting environment of healthcare today, the pharmaceutical industry has allowed the medicines we offer to be painted as part of the problem instead of as part of the solution. Clearly, we need to do a better job of explaining the *value* of prescription drugs, and also *developing* increasingly valuable medicines.

Somehow over the last 30 years, considerations of the cost and price of prescription medicines have completely overshadowed the issue of value. Maybe a short review of these economic concepts is in order at this point. A company calculates the *cost* of a medicine. (The cost is the amount of money we spend to produce it.) It determines the *price* of the medicine. (The price is the financial exchange for providing the medicine). But *value* is determined not by a company, but by its customers. In a free market economy, the value of a medicine is precisely what customers believe the medicine is worth to them.

Here is the example I often use to demonstrate the difference between price and value. If you took the 10 top-selling drugs of 1993 and looked at their wholesale prices, the average price per prescription was $44 per month.[3] For most Americans, $44 a month is not a huge burden. Many of us spend more than that on our cell phones.

What do you think would be the average price per prescription of the same drugs today? Sixty dollars? One hundred dollars? No, the answer is eleven dollars per prescription. That's because nine out of ten of these drugs are now off-patent and available at the lower costs that generics command. That's the nature of pharmaceutical pricing. They start out at one level while they are patented, but eventually they lose their patents, they are copied, and prices plunge. Outside of computers, I don't know of too many industries where a decade later the same product can be bought for discounts of more than 75 percent.

When the pharmaceutical industry does its job and introduces innovative products on a reliable basis, patients are enamored by the promise and power of new medicines. The focus shifts from the cost of drugs to the benefits and value they deliver. I'm thinking now of outrage associated with the high cost of Viagra when it was introduced in 1996. In fact, the price of Viagra was the one thing not on anyone's minds. The mechanism of Viagra was so novel, its effectiveness so compelling for men who had given up hope, that the only thing people saw was value.

There are many ways to express the value of medicines. Many diseases that once represented death sentences have been transformed into treatable chronic conditions. Only 40 years ago, heart disease incapacitated millions of Americans; today, medicine lets people living with the condition have routine lives.

Another way to demonstrate the value of medicines is to ask the following hypothetical question. In 1980, healthcare spending on medicines was about $52 a year per person (adjusted for inflation). Today, the average American spends nearly $504 on medicines per year.[4] Suppose I offered you that difference of $452 in the form of a check. Would you take it, if in exchange you could have only the medications that were available in 1980? I suspect that most of us would turn down the cash because we want what's behind Door Number One—better medicines.

This same trend in spending allows for a less charitable interpretation. Perhaps this large increase in drug spending actually demonstrates how overmedicated Americans have become. This is one of the reasons for the perception that the pharmaceutical industry is profiteering at the expense of the American consumer. While it's true that more Americans are being prescribed more medicines, I don't think it's fair to characterize the situation as *over*medication. *Appropriate* medication is the goal I hope doctors are working toward. In the last 20 years, the *intensity* of prescription drug use has also increased. Intensity is a measure of the application of drugs as a result of higher rates of early diagnosis and more aggressive treatment of chronic diseases.

The truth is Americans are being prescribed more prescription drugs than ever before. About 40 percent of Americans use at lease one prescription medication, and 17 percent use three or more, according to the Centers for Disease Control and Prevention.[5] Both figures represent big increases from just five years ago. Nor can these increases be explained by an aging population. The figures are age adjusted. People are simply taking more drugs, regardless of age group.

Take the case of asthma medications. During the last 20 years, physicians have been much more aggressive in their attempts to prevent asthma attacks. As a result, the average person struggling with asthma went from filling about 9 to 14 prescriptions a year. This is the result of doctors not only increasing the intensity of asthma medications but also an adjustment in what's called the therapeutic mix. In an attempt to fight the disease more effectively, doctors are switching many of their patients to newer, better, and more expensive drugs.

Many healthcare agencies that administer Medicaid complain that they spend more money on asthma medications than any other category of drugs. That's because asthma is epidemic among the young, lower-income families that Medicaid covers. But until we find a cure for asthma (we're working on it) or until society invests in better housing, the best we can do is to treat the symptoms. It is simply more cost-effective for society to treat the symptoms of diseases such as asthma, diabetes, and AIDS with medicine than with hospitalization.

That brings me to the hard reason why prescription drugs are so expensive: they cost a lot of time and money to discover and develop. I wish we could develop medicines cheaper and faster, so they could be priced lower and more people could readily afford them. Towards this goal, I am sorry to admit that the industry, including Pfizer, has lately failed to deliver a level of innovation that people have come to expect from us. Perhaps that expectation is part of the problem. Despite our best efforts to streamline the R&D process, it still takes 10-12 years and $1 billion or more to put a new medicine into the hands of physicians. Even when we seem to get it right and a drug becomes successful at helping many people, new clinical information can sweep the ground from under it.

That's why I think we can do better than the industry's traditional defense of high drug prices. That argument goes like this: "Yes, prescription drugs are expensive, but that just goes to show that they must have real value. We must charge high prices because prescription drugs are very costly to develop and we need to recover those costs. We are doing our job as innovative research-based companies delivering a steady stream of powerful medicines that add to the quality and length of life and avert even more expensive medical care. The high cost of prescription drugs is the price of entry to participate in the American free-enterprise system that provides such benefits."

That argument might have worked 25 years ago, but I don't think my industry has kept its part of the bargain. If the industry were innovating at the rate it was 25 years ago, I don't think there would be as many complaints about costs. If we announced tomorrow a cure for cancer, I think the resulting jubilation would effectively end the pricing issue.

The truth is that despite our very best efforts, the pace of delivering truly innovative drugs has slowed down. We have yet to deliver, for example, on the genomic revolution that allows us to peer into the very building blocks of disease.

The 1950s opened a fertile time of innovation for the pharmaceutical industry, one that lasted nearly 30 years. We turned the polio vaccine from a laboratory curiosity into a medicine that wiped out a multigenerational threat. We helped usher in the Age of Antibiotics with medicines like penicillin and Terramycin. Over the next three decades, the research-based pharmaceutical industry discovered class after class of new medicines. If you open your medicine cabinet today, most of what you'll find—antacids, antidepressants, anti-inflammatory medicines, antihistamines, and blood pressure medicine—came out of this fertile period.

But that was then, and this is now. Perhaps we picked the low-hanging fruit, and new discoveries are now that much more difficult. Or maybe the decisions we made 10 years ago, to go for "home runs" in terms of new therapies, turned out to be the wrong choices. For whatever reason, the pace of innovation has slowed. Too frequently we put our R&D dollars on the wrong horse and abandon a compound after investing hundreds of millions of dollars and years of work. When this happens, and it happens more frequently than any of us prefer, what I lament most is the loss of opportunity. While we were chasing one molecule, perhaps a more promising entity had to wait. At the same time, I am encouraged by recent developments. This progress is due to significant changes in the way we now approach pharmaceutical research and development. I discuss these changes in Chapter 10.

Are Drug Prices Really That High?

Pharmaceutical costs right now are in the spotlight. People believe that drug costs are one of the largest, if not the largest, driver of recent double-digit increases in healthcare costs. Is this a valid conclusion?

Forty years ago, the cost of medicines as a percent of total healthcare spending in the United States was about 10 percent. The percentage is about the same today. For every dollar spent on healthcare, around 10 cents goes for medications, as compared to more than 30 percent for hospitals and more than 25 percent for doctors.

At least one thing has changed. While the percentage of spending on drugs remains at the levels of the 1960s, medicines are now the largest component of healthcare purchased directly by consumers. Today, we are digging deeper into our pockets to pay for medications. We are using more medicines, and, thanks to the cost-shifting I discussed earlier, copays are getting larger. Naturally, we are more sensitive to payments we make out of our own pockets than the much larger payments made by insurance companies on our behalf to doctors and hospitals. Even in the 79 percent of the time in 2000 (up from 19 percent in 1993) that prescription medicines are covered by insurance, copayments for brand-name prescription medicines have increased from an average of $8.70 in 1997 to $14.11 in 2000 to $16.75 in 2003.[6]

This change in out-of-pocket spending on prescriptions colors people's perceptions. About half of Americans believe that pharmaceutical costs represent the largest contributor to overall healthcare costs.

Recently one of my friends had a heart attack. The bill for Ed's (not his real name) hospitalization was more than $50,000, which his insurance company paid. When Ed left the hospital, he had to pay about $1500 to cover his deductible and some optional services provided by the hospital—cable TV, long-distance phone calls, and the like. He also had a prescription to fill to help him prevent a second heart attack. The cost of this medicine was about three dollars a day. Guess what Ed complained about? The total hospital bill? His copay? No, as far as Ed was concerned, the pharmaceutical industry became the sharp edge of the blame game about healthcare costs. He didn't write the check for the $50,000 hospital bill. He probably never even saw it, nor did he focus on the bills submitted for the team of medical professionals who saved his life. But the $100 Ed has to pull out of his pocket every month is a constant irritant.

It's time for new thinking. Efforts by governments and insurance companies to control total healthcare spending by pounding drug prices into the ground are self-defeating. Germany, for example, has now gone through a half decade of healthcare reform. Every year, the German health ministry uses price controls to ratchet down the price of prescription medicines. Thanks to price controls, prescription medications now represent 3.6 percent of total German healthcare spending. When I met recently with Germany's economic minister I asked, "What are you going to do now? After five years, you've made drug spending such an insignificant part of total healthcare spending that you could now make the medicines free and it wouldn't materially impact the healthcare budget." Meanwhile, Germany's hospital costs are going through the roof, while Germans do not have enough access to modern medicines.

Criticizing the cost of drugs alone without also considering quality and value does not do this important subject justice. The costs of today's best medicines might be high, but the roots of angioplasty or coronary bypass surgery are vastly more expensive. What patient would not prefer medication to invasive surgery? The difference between the price of pharmaceutical therapy and the price of surgical intervention represents real value to both the patient and society. It's better in the short term and cheaper in the long term to prevent heart attacks and strokes than to treat them.

Our critics complain that prescription pharmaceuticals represent too high a percentage of total healthcare spending. But there's another way to think about this.

Imagine a world in which prescription pharmaceuticals represented the vast majority of healthcare costs, and hospitals and nursing homes represented very little. Is this a world you would like your children to inherit? I would be delighted to have my children and grandchildren regard open heart surgery the same way we now think of surgery for stomach ulcers. Every medical condition would be prevented or alleviated by an effective and appropriate pharmacological therapy. It would be a world without hospitals, operating rooms, and X-ray machines. Spending on medical devices, artificial hearts, artificial hips, and heart–lung bypass machines would be relics of a primitive past. The truth is, the more aggressively we can treat diseases with medicines, the more money we can save by preventing far more expensive invasions and interventions. Seen in this light, perhaps pharmaceuticals represent too *low* a percentage of total healthcare spending.

The U.S. pharmaceutical industry is also criticized for being the industry with the highest profits. The implication is that we should lower product prices and settle for lower profits. I can only say that profits enable us to consolidate the time, capital, and talent needed to create new medicines.

While it's true that the pharmaceutical industry has consistently earned top-tier profits relative to other industries, beginning in 2002 it slipped to fourth place behind mining, crude-oil production, and commercial banking.[7] Some critics will dispute these figures, so for the sake of argument, let's agree that drug company profits remain the highest of all industries. By definition, one industry or another must be the nation's most profitable. What industry would you choose to be at the top of the list? Gold mines? Off-shore drilling? Investment banking? Or advanced pharmaceuticals?

Pharmaceutical research is a reflection of the creative vitality of a modern nation. I believe it is possible to measure the creative momentum of a country on the basis of its support for pharmaceutical research. By that measure, the United States has it right. Our children will be beneficiaries of the jobs, intellectual energy, and medical innovations that are flowing to the United States.

The Fallacy of Recapturing R&D Costs

Defenders of the pharmaceutical industry typically trot out a standard reason why prescription medicines are as expensive as they are. I'll mention this reason, but briefly, and only to dismiss it for a reason I think is much stronger.

The common assertion is that prescription drugs are costly because the drug companies need to recover the high costs of research and development that went into their development. The industry has used a figure of $800 million as the average cost of bringing a pharmaceutical compound through screening, chemistry, preclinical development, and clinical testing. Our critics say we exaggerate these numbers. Can we agree that it's a number with a lot of zeros after it, and however many zeros there are, it's quite irrelevant?

It's a fallacy to suggest that our industry, or any industry, prices a product to recapture the R&D budget spent in development. Business doesn't work like that. Those are sunk costs. In other words, we spent the money and it cannot be recovered no matter what we decide to do with pricing. Incremental costs are different, and we can talk about them. But for pricing considerations, sunk costs are irrelevant. If we let sunk costs influence our decisions, we would not be evaluating a pricing decision exclusively on the merits of its own business case. Pricing decisions should be based on future possibilities, not biased by 10-year-old decisions. We must look ahead, using the past as a compass, but not an anchor.

If we don't use sunk costs to determine the price of medicines, how do we decide what to charge? It's basically the same as pricing a car, a consumer product, or an appliance. What will it take to sustain investors' confidence in the risk and rewards of an industry? A number of factors go into the mix. These factors consider cost of business, competition, patent status, anticipated volume, and, most important, our estimation of the income generated by sales of the product. It is the anticipated income stream, rather than repayment of sunk costs, that is the primary determinant of price.

We use the income to do three things. First, like you, Pfizer uses income to pay its bills. Second, the income funds new R&D, so we can introduce innovative new medicines, making the company more valuable to everyone from patients to investors. And third, we use the income to pay dividends to our shareholders, who originally invested money to develop the medicine in the first place. If we generate more income, more investors desire to invest in our company, and the price of our stock goes up. If we don't generate sufficient income in the eyes of our investors, then the reverse will occur. Investors will shift their capital to companies that can put it to more productive use, our stock will go down, and we'll have less capital with which to work.

It's a brutal system for participants, but in the long run it's good for the country because there is no better way to determine priorities and allocate resources where they will bring the most benefit to the most people.

The system also benefits patients. It means that we must be innovative or our century-and-a-half legacy as an independent company will end. That's a powerful incentive to invest in new medicines. When I joined Pfizer 35 years ago, it was by general consensus regarded as a well-managed but third-tier pharmaceutical company. Today it is by the same measures counted as the leading company in its sector. I am very pleased with this achievement, but I also know that history has a way of humbling front-runners. If I ever need a reminder, all I have to do is peruse the list of the world's top 10 pharmaceutical companies from just 30 years ago. In 1975, the top 10 pharmaceutical companies in the world were:

Leading Pharmaceutical Firms by Country of Origin—1975[8]

	Name	Country
1.	Roche	Switzerland
2.	Hoechst/Roussel	Germany
3.	Merck	United States
4.	Ciba-Geigy	Switzerland
5.	Lilly	United States
6.	American Home Products	United States
7.	Warner-Lambert	United States
8.	Sandoz	Switzerland
9.	Pfizer	United States
10.	Boehringer-Ingelheim	Germany

Leading Pharmaceutical Firms by Country of Origin—2004[9]

	Name	Country
1.	Pfizer	United States
2.	Johnson & Johnson	United States
3.	GlaxoSmithKline	United Kingdom
4.	Novartis	Switzerland
5.	Roche Group	Switzerland
6.	Merck	United States
7.	Bristol-Myers Squibb	United States
8.	Aventis	France
9.	Abbott Laboratories	United States
10.	AstraZeneca	United Kingdom

What a difference a few decades makes. Of the 10 largest pharmaceutical firms in 1975, only two remain on the list in 2004.[10] Four are no longer in existence. If history is a guide, 30 years from now the list of top 10 pharmaceutical firms will be unrecognizable.

None of the companies on the list today have a guarantee. Companies have to earn their place on the list every day. If they falter, the market eventually replaces them with others. If there's one trend that I think we can bank on, though, is that U.S.-based pharmaceutical companies will continue to dominate the list. That's largely a result of U.S. free-market policies that have made it a beacon for the best in biomedical science. That leadership accrues to the benefit of workers (we create five jobs outside our industry for every one we create inside it). It also advantages American patients, who benefit from the world's most dynamic and successful industry—an industry of the future.

The Drug and the Physician

Let me draw a comparison between the process of developing a drug and the process of developing the physician who prescribes the drug. Society values both doctors and medicines. In both cases, society makes an up-front investment in order to acquire intellectual property that is protected by a government license. In the case of pharmaceuticals, we invest in R&D in order to secure an exclusive patent. No one else can lawfully sell that drug during the life of the patent, and the prices tend to be high.

In the case of physicians, we invest in expensive medical schools in order to train doctors. Society then licenses physicians, giving them the legal right to provide certain services, such as diagnosing disease and prescribing medicine. No one but licensed physicians can lawfully provide such services, and the prices tend to be high.

Physicians set their fees in part to generate enough income to pay for their up-front investment in the intellectual property they have acquired. Most physicians pay a lot of money to attend medical school. Others have to take on huge loans. Even so, the costs for medical school are subsidized by a variety of private and government mechanisms. If we made medical students pay the true costs of their training, most of them couldn't afford it. We simply wouldn't have enough doctors entering the profession without the subsidies. The final part of the equation is the government license. Few doctors would enter the profession without the government license that limits competition and keeps fees high enough to justify their investment in acquiring the intellectual property required to be a doctor.

We can do a thought experiment about lowering doctors' fees. What would happen if we passed a law that arbitrarily reduced doctors' fees? The consequence would mirror the effect on investors of lowering returns on investment. Just as investors would seek out more financially rewarding investments, talented students would seek out more financially rewarding professions. Why should students make such a risky investment in their training if they could make the same salary in another occupation that did not require such an investment?

A thought experiment with respect to pharmaceutical companies has the same outcome. What would happen if we passed a law that arbitrarily reduced drug prices? Investors would seek greener pastures. Why would anyone make a 10-12 year investment in pharmaceutical R&D if they could get the same return in another industry that presented much less risk to their capital? Research-based drug companies would cease to make long-term investments in new medicines. The immediate impact to society would not be obvious—it's difficult to miss something that was never introduced—but our children's health would suffer from possibilities squandered by their parents.

Those who believe that these are scare tactics can visit countries such as France, Germany, or Italy and see for themselves. Only a few years ago, Central Europe was known as the "Medicine Chest of the World." Europe today stands for a patchwork of price controls, formulary restrictions, product diversions, intentional gaps in patient information, and mandated intrusions into the relationships between patients and their doctors. Germany loses tens of thousands of pharmaceutical jobs every year. Europeans often wait years for medicines routinely available in the United States.

Branded Prescription Drugs and Generics

Branded drug prices are anywhere from 25-100 percent more expensive in the United States than in countries such as England, France, and Canada. That's the reality.

But this is true only for branded drugs under patent protection. Critics of the industry look only at this one class of drugs. There is another side. Exactly the reverse of the pricing situation occurs in the generic-drug marketplace. Prices of generic drugs in the United States are lower than anywhere else in the world. No country even comes close to having generic drug prices as low as in the United States.

This shouldn't be surprising. Competition works. Generic drugs, also called off-patent drugs, enter the market when a company's patent protection expires. Because there are so many generic drug companies in the United States that step in to make drugs once their patent protection ends, and because these drug makers have virtually no R&D costs, generic drugs here are the cheapest in the world.

In other words, Americans pay more for drugs when they first come out and less for generic drugs, while the rest of the world pays less for patented drugs and more for generics. Why are the situations reversed? Because government price controls on drugs distort the picture, introduce inefficiencies, and destroy incentives needed for a robust research-based pharmaceutical industry. Branded drugs are largely supplied by global companies whose main operations are in the United States. Generic drug companies tend to be local. Are we surprised that generic drug prices are higher outside of the United States?

The good news for consumers is that every branded drug will eventually have a generic version. I'd rather shop in a country where there is robust competition, and where generic drugs cost much less than in other countries. In the United States, so many blockbuster drugs have gone off-patent recently that the rate of increase in drug spending in the United States has dropped for the past five years.

Which system is better for consumers? I believe consumers are better served by a free-market system that supports strong research-based companies introducing many products that compete fiercely in every market segment. Consumers might pay more for a portfolio of new drugs, but they will eventually pay less for a much larger and growing portfolio of generic medicines.

Within the first year after a company's patent expires, it loses up to 90 percent of its market share to low-priced alternatives crowding the market. There are dozens of generic drug manufacturing companies with a red circle around June 28, 2011. That's the day the patent for our anti-cholesterol medication Lipitor expires. Shortly thereafter, a number of generic alternatives to Lipitor will be introduced and consumers will have a choice of generic tablets containing atorvastatin calcium, the active ingredient of Lipitor. Based on experience with other drugs whose patents have expired, Pfizer can expect in the following year to lose 90 percent of revenue for that drug as the market switches to generic versions.

Without the property rights that patents affirm, the private research-based drug industry could not exist. Sometimes I make my point with this analogy. Suppose that you are a farmer. Would you plant crops if you could not be assured that others would be excluded from reaping them? Without property rights, we'd still be hunters and gatherers. Intellectual property rights are so important they are enshrined in the Constitution of the United States. Those who risk their assets to bring new drugs into being must receive the rewards available for successful ventures.

Protected by our patent, we use the money generated by our exclusive right to sell Lipitor to generate enough income to pay the investors who funded the research costs, and to pay for the next round of research. Our goal is to replace the income stream we lose when the patent for Lipitor expires with another life-saving medicine or group of medicines. We hope that forthcoming medicine, in turn, will enable us to deliver even more products. The market will tell us if we will meet this goal, but that's okay. The real sin for us is if we miss an opportunity. In the long run—the only way to view this business—this is the bargain we believe is best for patients.

This bargain benefits society in a number of ways. By filing the patent, innovators give the world complete information about new products. When the patent expires, competitors can use that information to make generic versions of the product. They can charge lower prices because they never incur the costs of development and testing. Again, that's good for everybody. Generic manufacturers have an important role to play in the healthcare of Americans. It's because of generic manufacturers competing for market share that the prices of top-selling medicines are a fraction of what they were 10 years earlier.

Contrary to media perception, we in the branded pharmaceutical business have no problem with generic competition. We understand the reality—patents don't last forever. Our problems are with generic companies that steal or ignore patents, or who file patent challenge after patent challenge with the goal of damaging a rightfully earned patent. This adds cost for all patents and undermines a system that has paid enormous dividends for patients awaiting new treatments.

CHAPTER 5

WHY DOES THE INDUSTRY DO SO MUCH MARKETING?

The bulk of the pharmaceutical industry's "marketing" budgets go to supporting professional representatives charged with the task of informing physicians about the products they represent. The reality is that in almost every therapeutic category, physicians have a choice of pharmaceuticals to prescribe. Our responsibility is to make sure the physician has complete information about the Pfizer product he or she prescribes. Our competitors have field representatives too, and their job is to bring the information about their products to the attention of the same physicians.

Most physicians welcome field representatives. Doctors, who are too busy to read all the literature on new drugs, value the briefings they received from company representatives. Our professionals often earn doctors' time because they bring timely, useful scientific data on their drugs. The free samples delivered to doctors' offices help patients, particularly those with no insurance coverage for prescription drugs. Some Medicare patients can get all the drugs they need from samples. But as managed care put relentless pressure on physicians to see more patients per day, some doctors began to see drug company representatives as intrusions.

The numbers suggest that doctors are exhausted by all the various companies' representatives calling on them. It's not just from drug companies, either. Mixed in with the patients in the waiting room are representatives for medical devices, healthcare equipment, and diagnostic services. The doctors are increasingly slamming the door on all representatives. The average representative had 808 meetings with doctors in 1996. By 2001, the average representative met with only 529 doctors. A recent McKinsey

& Co. study found that only one in every five sales calls results in a conversation with a doctor. Often these calls are less than five minutes long.[1]

Why do we do it? Experience shows that face-to-face talks to doctors are more effective than printed information in getting doctors to understand more about our medicines and to consider prescribing our products, when appropriate, for their patients. Yet it's an expensive and often frustrating process. Often when one company's representatives succeed in persuading a doctor to consider prescribing their company's product, representatives from a competing drug company are waiting to talk to the doctor about their product. Perhaps there is a better way to do all this, but doctors want to know "what's new?" in medicines, and this is how we can answer that question, and others physicians may have.

Some say that prescription drugs are priced as high as they are because the pharmaceutical industry spends so much money on marketing and advertising. If the industry would just limit its advertising budget, critics suggest, drug prices would fall.

It seems to me that the better accusation is not that the industry does too much marketing, but that it is lousy at the marketing it does. I'm the first one to question the sums that Pfizer budgets for marketing. To paraphrase advertising pioneer David Ogilvy, half of all marketing expenditures is wasted. The trouble is, no one knows which half. If someone can show me that the resources going to marketing can be more effectively spent elsewhere, that's where they will go.

When patients write me about Pfizer's marketing practices, they generally focus on the television advertisements we run for our branded pharmaceutical products. Less frequently, I'm asked about the magazine and newspaper advertising. Few people ask me about the main expenditure in our marketing budget—educating and otherwise serving the healthcare professionals who prescribe our products. A smaller yet more visible component of the marketing budget goes to what the industry calls Direct-to-Consumer (DTC) advertising and what I prefer to call DTC education.

Direct-to-Consumer Advertising

When I was a child, our family physician was straight out of a Norman Rockwell painting. Smart, bordering on all-knowing, our family doctor was compassionate, yet authoritative. He told us what to do and we did it. I suspect most people my age have similar recollections.

Over the past few decades, the world has changed. People want more control over their lives, and they prefer to be in partnership with their healthcare professionals. In every aspect of our lives, from the retirement options available to us to the tunes loaded in our iPods, we demand choice. In exchange, we have agreed to be more engaged in areas of our lives many of us have been content to let others direct. Today, in our careers, our consumer purchases, and our healthcare, we expect to be more informed, engaged, and involved.

A consequence of this change is that patients now play a much more active role in their health than they ever did. Increasingly, they view themselves as partners with their doctors in healthcare decisions. This fundamental shift is an important step and a healthy one, as neither patients nor doctors can do their jobs in isolation. Doctors can diagnose patients and tell them how to get better or stay healthy. But patients must be the ones to make the recommendations work.

Enter DTC advertising of pharmaceutical medicines. We know that patients want to be empowered with information to make better decisions, in partnership with their doctors, about their health. The key goals of most DTC ads are to inform people about a disease or condition, raise awareness of available treatment options, and prompt patients to talk to their doctors. If we've accomplished that, we've succeeded.

DTC outreach is a relatively recent phenomenon for the drug industry. In 1997, the Food and Drug Administration (FDA) eased restrictions on TV ads for prescription drugs. I supported this change in America because I believe that patients empowered by information are better prepared to participate in the healthcare decisions that concern them and their families. In general, I believe that patients are empowered by more rather than less access to information. DTC advertising reflects the reality that Americans are among the world's most demanding consumers and that a higher level of awareness about healthcare options is a positive development.

Yet the practice of DTC advertising has many critics who say that the industry's spending on DTC drives up prices, leads to overprescribing or inappropriate prescribing, and undermines the doctor-patient relationship.

Most of the criticisms aren't backed by survey evidence. In fact, surveys show the opposite. Five out of six patients motivated to talk with their doctors about a DTC ad were far more interested in learning about the options than requesting a specific therapy, reports the National Consumer League. According to the FDA, 93 percent of patients say their doctors welcome their questions about drugs advertised on TV or through print.

This is not to say that DTC advertising is perfect. I think there are legitimate differences about how these ads communicate risk. I'll speak to all the common criticisms of DTC advertising, but let me start with what I believe is good about DTC. There are very clear public health benefits to DTC. Our ads have prompted millions of people to talk to their doctors about a health concern, many for the first time. Nearly nine out of ten patients, according to the FDA, had the condition highlighted in the ad. A Harvard Medical School survey showed that about 25 percent of the time, doctors made a totally new diagnosis based on the discussion—often for a "high priority" condition such as hypertension, diabetes, or high cholesterol. When done well, DTC ads can motivate patients to get and stay healthy, and improve our healthcare system.

I believe DTC is an area in which our business interests are clearly aligned with the public good. We want people to know we have a product that, if their doctor decides it is right for them, may help them stay healthy. We need patients to talk to their doctors to get the appropriate diagnosis. People have to find out how they can manage their disease or condition—whether through lifestyle changes or some form of treatment, or both. The doctor and patient get to decide what, if any, lifestyle change, treatment, or medicine is appropriate.

Our research with doctors and patients tells us that this is how the process works. Take our ads for Viagra. Millions of men went to see their doctors based on those commercials, which highlighted erectile dysfunction. In talking with their doctors, many of those men discovered they had hypertension or high cholesterol. Their doctors diagnosed them, and the patients got appropriate treatments. In this way, DTC has saved lives, and I'm proud of that track record.

Now, let me speak to the critics and their issues.

First, prices. DTC does not raise prices. We set prices based on the value the drugs deliver to patients. We do not draw up a budget that outlines how much we're going to spend on DTC and make sure we recoup that money in sales. Studies show there's no correlation between prices or price increases and DTC advertising. A study of top-selling prescription medicines by the National Institute for Health Care Management showed that the average price of drugs that are advertised is lower than those that aren't.[2]

Inextricable from concerns about pricing are the personal issues of access and affordability. I believe that Pfizer has the best programs for low-income and uninsured patients in the industry, programs that offer these patients access to Pfizer medicines at prices ranging from the heavily discounted to free of charge. Millions of people in America can qualify to get Pfizer medicines at no cost, or for a small dispensing fee. I'd be thrilled if everyone who could take part in our access programs actually did.

These kinds of programs are available from most of the companies in our industry, and, overall, we're doing a better job of publicizing its access programs. But we can do better, and we must. These programs address a key barrier–cost–that prevents many people from following their doctor's advice, and we need to make sure the people who need those programs are aware of them.

But another barrier is information. And here DTC advertising can play a role, an educational role.

Second, DTC does not drive *over*prescribing. Despite years of DTC advertising, Americans remain *under*treated for a number of serious conditions. For example, if all physicians followed the NIH's treatment guidelines, the number of Americans being treated for hypertension would rise from 20 million to 43 million, and the number of Americans taking cholesterol-lowering treatments, such as Lipitor or one of the "statin" drugs, would increase by a factor of 10. "By these measures, it doesn't seem that we are spending too much on prescription drugs," writes Malcolm Gladwell in *The New Yorker*. "If the federal government's own medical researchers are to be believed, we're spending too little."[3]

You can see the challenge here. I would argue that through DTC advertising, we've done a very good job of raising consumer awareness that these health conditions exist, and informing patients that they can do something about those conditions. We've also made a lot of progress through our outreach on public health issues, such as cardiovascular risk and depression.

The problem, we've realized, is that information isn't enough. When it comes to health, there are a host of serious barriers that prevent people from doing what they need to do to improve their lives. Why does anyone today smoke cigarettes? Are there still adults who do not accept that tobacco use is bad for their health? Shouldn't everyone have quit by now, based on what we know about the health effects of smoking? We know that most smokers want to quit, but have failed, some many times. Clearly, despite a wealth of available information about prevention and wellness, many people who should take action on their health choose not to, or can't change an ingrained habit.

One of the goals of our DTC ads has been to address those emotional or attitudinal barriers to choosing positive health behaviors. Here's one barrier our research has uncovered. Many people just don't want to take medicine because doing so makes them feel "old," "sick," or "weak." DTC communications have increasingly focused on helping such people seek treatment despite these internal, emotional barriers. However, we need to pay more attention to ensuring that they understand the risks of medications. Good DTC advertising does both. We must remember the need to support the doctor's role as healthcare partner. And we must clearly communicate about the risks that come with any medicine.

If in the process of trying to motivate people to act on their health, we feed the impression that there is, as some critics say, "a pill for every ill," then we are doing a disservice to the millions of Americans who need something other than a pill for what ails them—such as a lifestyle change or some other treatment. This is a very difficult issue. Clearly, we need to inform and motivate. At the same time, we should not make taking our medicines so attractive that it discourages consumers from considering other options, including lifestyle changes.

In the end, when I need to decide on what level of information should be presented, my instinct is to err on the side of more rather than less.

In the rush to condemn DTC advertising, many critics seemingly forget that the doctor still is the ultimate decision maker; no matter how much or how well a pharmaceutical company advertises its products to consumers, the physician still must write the prescription. For that reason, the industry needs to do a better job of supporting the physician. One way to support the physician is to include specific language in DTC advertising, making clear that there may be alternative therapies available for the disease being discussed. This includes non-drug alternatives like improved diet and exercise. Adding this information will help to reinforce the importance of a productive physician-patient conversation to improving patient health.

Finally, we need to step up to a reality that everyone today understands much more completely than they did even a short time ago: every medicine carries with it a degree of benefit and risk. Drug companies can comply with FDA advertising requirements, but if every drug ad says, "this drug may give you headaches," at some point we risk having our discussions about side effects become "white noise." We're doing research with patient and consumer groups on the subject of risk communications that I hope will give the industry and regulators some valuable guidance on how people interpret messages about risk. I want each of our ads to be tailored to ensure that those messages are heard and understood.

We need to be up-front about risk. The fact is that every drug has risks, and no drug, not even aspirin, is 100-percent safe or appropriate for everyone. Doctors and patients must consider the risk of any medicine against the anticipated benefit. This risk/benefit analysis will differ by patient and by disease. One patient who lives in chronic pain might be willing to accept a small risk of a serious side effect for a medicine that effectively deals with that pain; for another patient, such a risk would be unacceptable. Only the patient and doctor, working together, can make the right decision for that patient. In today's risk-intolerant environment, some appear to argue that no risk is acceptable. My perspective is that responsible, educated adults should have the opportunity to weigh risks and benefits with their physician.

I acknowledge that these are complex issues that we have not yet resolved. Despite all the good that DTC advertising has done in terms of patient empowerment and awareness, I think it's time for change. In Chapter 13, I outline four specific areas that companies like Pfizer can address to add more value to DTC information—and to ensure that we offer a marketing and educational approach that distinctively benefits patients, physicians, and the healthcare system that serves us all.

CHAPTER 6

WHY DO AMERICANS PAY MORE THAN CANADIANS FOR DRUGS?

The question, in its infinite varieties, comes at me more often than the others.

I recognize that it's irresistible to look to Canada as a solution to high prescription drug prices in the United States. But sometimes I don't know what to make of it. The idea of drug importation invokes a society in which we have vague notions about cost and value, cause and effect, responsibility and desire—where both the economic and moral superstructure that fits all of these concepts together has been swept away.

It's important to note that not *all* medicines in Canada are priced lower than they are in the United States. Generic drugs are actually priced far higher. What's priced lower—and what gets all the attention—are "branded" pharmaceuticals that are under patent.

Branded medicines aren't priced lower in Canada because of some natural advantage inherent in Canadian pharmacies. *Prices* in Canada are lower than U.S. prices because the Canadian government caps the amount that U.S. pharmaceutical companies can charge Canadian pharmacies, distributors, and wholesalers. Those lower wholesale prices mean lower retail prices for Canadians compared to what Americans pay. But the cost of a branded medicine, whether consumed in the United States, Canada, or anywhere else, is the same.

Of course, we can always refuse to sell other countries our products and try to "force" market prices on the world. But sovereign countries that balk at market prices have a variety of tactics they can apply. The reality is that once pharmaceutical companies have sunk the research costs necessary to develop medicines, governments often use their power as regulators, dominant purchasers, and arbiters of intellectual property rights to enforce their demands. For example, a government displeased with free-market prices could simply license local manufacturers to produce the drug. It's a powerful threat, and the governments know it. As big and influential as some drug companies may be, we can't fight sovereign nations.

So we give in. We don't like it, but as long as governments are willing to pay more than our costs of manufacturing the drug, we go ahead and sell to them fearing that the alternative is worse. But there is one condition of this arrangement: that the drugs we send to such countries are consumed locally and not exported.

Prescription medicines cost a lot to invent and somebody has to pay for it. For the past 20 years, that burden has fallen largely on the people of the United States. I call for that burden to be shared more equally by the millions of people around the world who benefit from the risk and investment that went into developing medicines. That's a tough road upwards, but the answer isn't to arbitrarily reduce the prices in the United States.

Drug prices don't have to be as high as they are for people in the United States. It's time for freer markets in Canada, Europe, and other developed nations. This is a matter of simple fairness that lies at the heart of free trade. Yet price controls on branded medicines exist around the world. These price controls are ultimately destructive to the quest for lower costs. Whatever narrow interests they might advance, price controls always make prices higher in the long run. It's time for price controls to end and for industries to put their efforts into developing new or better products. In the long run, the people of the world would be better off without them. Starting with pharmaceuticals, I call for price controls to be lifted in Canada and elsewhere. Let's work to keep price controls out of the United States and to tear them down around the world.

There's a worldwide market for medicines, but the United States pays the lion's share of the costs of developing new products. It's not only the world's largest economy, but it's also one of the most free. That freedom encourages innovation because investors are confident that the market will reward success. Is it any surprise that the United States is the source of most of the new, breakthrough medicines the rest of the world wants?

The United States is a blessed and generous country. Frankly, I think it is fair that Americans pay more for prescription drugs than people in developing countries in sub-Saharan Africa and parts of Asia and Latin America. I think we ought to subsidize those people who can't afford market prices. But I do not believe that we should be required to subsidize Canadians. It is time for Canadians and others to pay their fair share. To me, this isn't a health issue. It's a trade issue.

Free-Riding

When I was much younger, I had an acquaintance who figured out how to receive satellite cable TV without paying for it. He said that what he did really wasn't so bad because his actions did not add costs to the cable company and prevented no one else from using the system. My acquaintance was a classic free rider. The free-rider situation arises any time someone is able to consume a product or service without paying a fair share of the costs. The costs of the free rider don't disappear; they are just spread over those who do pay. Those who believe that importing drugs from Canada will help solve the problem of rising healthcare costs think they can make the United States a free rider on itself.

Rather than import drugs, let's be forthright and deal with the issue some people really want to import: price controls on drugs. Let's be honest and put the issue of price controls on the table and look at the pros and cons. I'm against price controls and I believe that importation of drugs is a distraction from the real issue of whether we as a society are willing to pay the high costs of developing new medicines. If we're not, let's have the decency to admit it.

And if we do impose price controls in the United States, let's not hide from the result. We would be ending the R&D process that brings forward new drugs, and pulling up the ladder of pharmaceutical innovation on those awaiting new treatments. We'd be telling our children and grandchildren, "We've got ours; sorry about yours." This is not the legacy I want to leave, but it's certainly more honest than the current debate on drug importation.

If we do have the debate about price controls, I imagine two proposals would emerge for reducing the price of prescription drugs in the United States. Both would irreparably damage the industry's ability to innovate.

Under the first proposal, the American government would imitate Canada's goal for lower drug prices by putting price controls on pharmaceuticals in America. Under the second proposal, the American government would become the sole buyer of drugs for the American market. Let me address each of these options.

If the first proposal succeeds, to quote Nobel Prize-winning economist Milton Friedman, "American consumers would get the short-term windfall of lower prices, but they would end up unnecessarily suffering and living shorter lives—because promising new therapies would be delayed or not even developed. Even the threat of price controls reduces the incentive to develop new drugs."[1]

In the real world, where nothing is free, the choice would be between low drug prices and innovation in new medicines. We cannot have both. If we actually tried importation from Canada on a large scale, we might save money for a while. But the bargain with the devil is this: we will have over the next 50 years the same number of drugs that Canadian pharmaceutical companies have developed since 1950. In the past I stated that this number was zero. But then I received a protest from the Canadian Consulate, which accused me of being unfair and distorting the record. In fact, as the economics minister pointed out, in 50 years the Canadian drug industry has actually brought two medicines to market. I stand corrected.

Under the second proposal, the U.S. government would become the sole buyer of drugs for the American market. By leveraging its massive buying power, the government would be able to command favorable rates from pharmaceutical companies. It could then either resell the drugs to pharmacies or dispense them through public clinics.

We already have experience with this model. The Department of Veterans Affairs, for example, negotiates on behalf of veteran healthcare drug coverage. The good news for veterans is that this approach works. Veterans pay less for drugs than other Americans. Now, I believe reduced drug prices to be one way a grateful society can honor the service of veterans, and I applaud it. But let's remember there is no free lunch. Someone else is paying a little more for this patriotic gesture.

de Facto Price Controls

If the purchasing power exercised by the Department of Veterans Affairs were extended to Medicare and Medicaid and beyond, we would have a *de facto* system of price controls. The federal government, in the interests of maximizing access to life-saving drugs, would use its power as dominant purchaser and arbiter of intellectual property rights to drive drug prices down. Government budgetary pressures, in effect, would dictate the price of medicines. That's why I supported language that limits the ability of the federal government to negotiate drug prices under the Medicare Prescription Drug, Improvement, and Modernization Act of 2003. Otherwise the pharmaceutical companies would end up having the same relationship with the federal government as do defense contractors. The government determines research priorities for the contractors to execute.

The real problems of government price controls show up in the unintended consequences, of which I see two.

It is a truism in economics that he who pays the bills ends up calling the shots. If the federal government buys the pills, decisions about the direction of pharmaceutical research would ultimately be driven by politics rather than medicine; the pharmaceutical research agenda would be set not by individual companies looking for a competitive edge, but by bureaucrats in Washington, DC. The government would decide which new drugs are worth developing. The result would be lower prices today and less innovation tomorrow. I don't think this is a trade-off most Americans would be willing to make.

Price controls on drugs, if imposed, would be vastly more difficult to rescind than other price controls. Controls on oil and other products often tend to be limited or short-lived because taxpayers eventually object to the shortages that result. The consequences of drug price controls are far more difficult to observe because they mainly affect medicines that haven't yet been invented. It's difficult to miss a product that you have never seen.

Even if people were to later realize that price controls were preventing new drugs from being developed, undoing the effects of those controls would be difficult. Ramping up a drug discovery effort would be complicated because patients would have to pay higher prices for years before they saw benefits. Drug companies would have to be convinced that controls would not be reimposed as soon as their new drugs are released.

I believe the present system offers the best opportunity to find balance between price and innovation. Since the virus that causes AIDS was identified 20 years ago, 82 medicines have been approved. Currently, pharmaceutical and biotechnology researchers are working toward the development of vaccines by testing 79 additional medicines for HIV/AIDS and related opportunistic infections.[2] Other new classes of drugs, available since 1993, are treating rheumatoid arthritis, Alzheimer's disease, Parkinson's disease, and high blood pressure.

The present system offers drug companies patent protection to give them a chance to reward investors, and fund the costs associated with the next round of developing and testing drugs. The result has been a major contribution to human health, longevity, and quality of life. Drug importation, price controls, and having the U.S. government negotiate prices with pharmaceutical companies would all have the same effect—they begin to unravel the returns that create incentives for innovation.

Importing Can't Meet America's Needs

Canada's pharmaceutical industry is an $8 billion industry. To put that in dramatic perspective, that's less than the annual worldwide sales of Lipitor. There are 16 million American patients on Lipitor alone; that's more than half of the entire Canadian population.

The State of Illinois recently passed a bill to import all of the drugs—about $2 billion worth—for the state's employees and Medicaid recipients. So Illinois proposes to reserve a quarter of the Canadian pharmaceutical industry for just one state. I don't think so.

Canadians are already starting to shut down the process. Health officials and patient advocacy groups north of the border are already taking action to clamp down on their own pharmacists and distributors to keep their drugs from going to the United States.

How could it be otherwise? If the Canadian government does nothing and keeps price controls at their current levels, Canadian wholesalers and retailers will prefer to sell drugs to Americans at higher prices rather than to Canadians at lower prices. Canadians will have trouble buying drugs in their own country. By the time this book comes out, I believe the drugs from Canada issue will be recognized as the distraction from the real issue that it really is.

Are Drugs from Canada Safe?

The pharmaceutical industry has cited safety concerns as the basis of its opposition to drug imports from Canada. In my speeches, I have echoed these concerns. But I fear that the safety issue the industry paints is too broad. Let me clarify my perspective.

Drugs from Canadian pharmacies are as safe as drugs from pharmacies in the United States. I have full confidence, for example, that Lipitor dispensed by a licensed pharmacist in Canada is genuine. I believe the same is true for other prescription and generic medicines dispensed by licensed pharmacies.

There is a critical safety issue with drugs sold through the Internet, whether the source purports to be Canadian or, as is likely, is actually from some ill-lit corner of the world. When the FDA and U.S. Customs Service inspected a random sample of 1153 imported drugs, 88 percent of them were deemed either counterfeit or not up to FDA standards. If you go to your mailbox and find the package of Lipitor you ordered over the Internet from a pharmacy that purports to be from

Canada, all bets are off. There is no reliable way to determine the origin or safety of those products.

When it comes to medicines, nothing is more important than product safety, so I want to be absolutely clear about this distinction. If you buy a Pfizer product in a licensed pharmacy in Canada, I can assure you to the best of my ability that it is safe. I believe drugs from other manufacturers are safe, as well. If you buy your meds on the Internet, there are no guarantees.

We Have It Backwards

We have the importation situation entirely backwards where the concern is focused on importing drugs from Canada, and questions of price controls and product safety and counterfeiting take center stage. Let's take a deep breath and examine the situation more closely.

The real issue is not the threat of importation; it's the threat to *exportation*. I'm talking about something much more fundamental than market segmentation or tinkering with the volume of drug products destined for sale in various parts of the world. The exportation I'm talking about concerns an intangible that affects the health of our children and our children's children more than any single medicine that Pfizer has developed.

The United States exports promise and hope. The promise is that old and new threats to health will not be left unchallenged by the largest research-based pharmaceutical infrastructure in the world. The hope is that our children will inherit a world that is just a little bit healthier than the world their mothers and fathers encountered.

It wasn't so long ago that mothers and fathers had a palpable fear of polio. Yet there are increasingly fewer of us who remember keeping our children home from the swimming pool or movie theater because of the fear of polio. How many readers have actually seen an iron lung in action? These monstrosities are relegated to museums and bad memories, courtesy of medicines that those who came before us left as their legacy.

Importation of lower-priced drugs from Canada and elsewhere threatens that promise because it undermines our ability to innovate. If we gutted our research-based pharmaceutical industry—and make no mistake about it, that would be the result of any importation strategy— we would break faith with the coming generations. What legacy will we have left our children? They would rightly accuse us of failure to honor their health as the people who came before us honored ours.

CHAPTER 7

WELCOME
COMPETITION
IN HEALTHCARE

Competition is the mother of lower costs and better quality. We rely on competition to keep prices down on everything we consume, from food to shoes to banking to laundry services. We know that there is but one force on earth that will motivate a seller to reduce its prices and improve quality: the near certainty that a competitor offering better prices or better quality will take away business.

Competition is good medicine for economies. Besides lowering costs, competition improves quality and encourages innovation. When one company introduces an innovation or superior process, it is copied by others. The bar keeps getting higher as one company's innovation quickly becomes the price of entry for others. Companies that refuse to adapt to the new standards of price and quality quickly exit the business, making room for new entrants. In this way, markets expand. Spurred by competition, entire industries become more transparent, distributing information (and power) more equally among buyers and sellers. Consumers end up with access to better data about prices, product specifications, and purchase outcomes.

Name an industry in which competition is allowed to flourish—computers, telecommunications, small package shipping, retailing, entertainment—and I'll show you lower prices, higher quality, more innovation, and better customer service. There's nary an exception.

Okay, there's one. So far, the healthcare industry seems immune to the discipline of competition. In every society, healthcare costs are high and rising. No amount of regulation seems to bring spending under control. In the meantime, healthcare services are restricted or rationed. Quality is problematic, with many patients receiving substandard care. Variability in costs, treatment approaches, and clinical outcomes threaten the integrity of the system. Preventable medical errors persist. Elements of the system actually resist innovation. Because players hoard information, the diffusion of best practices is slow. However you evaluate it, the healthcare systems of the world are not conforming to how an industry operates in a well-functioning, competitive market.

How can this be? Let's talk about the healthcare system in the United States, a system that seems to be subject to more competition than any other in the world. Participants such as physicians, hospitals, and insurance companies are predominantly private. And while it's true that the healthcare system is highly regulated, so are other industries, which to their dismay have not been immune to the laws of supply and demand. We would expect competition to slash costs in healthcare. Instead, healthcare costs keep rising. Has competition finally met its match?

Hardly. Competition remains the solution to the U.S. healthcare crisis, but it must be the right kind of competition. It's simply that competition in healthcare today operates on the wrong level. The players—health plans, payers, providers, and physicians—compete over the wrong things, at the wrong time, at the wrong places in the healthcare value chain. There's very little competition on the level where it really counts—at the level of the patient where tangible services are provided to real people. We need to adjust healthcare delivery in ways that will finally signal to participants that they must be accountable to the discipline of competition. Then we will see the benefits that boost every other industry.

Two quick stories illustrate how healthcare can respond to competition.

A CEO acquaintance of mine—let's call him Bob—decided that it was time to have the hip replacement surgery his doctor kept recommending. Bob prides himself on being an astute decision maker. Whether the item of interest is another company, a car, a vacation cruise, or a set of golf clubs, he analyzes balance sheets, costs, product reviews, customer testimonials, and other data before making a purchase decision. Yet when Bob sought the most basic information about one of the most significant decisions of his life, he was frustrated at every turn. His agenda was overwhelmed by the mysterious requirements of the system that treated him as a passive player. His choice of surgeons was limited. Before he could act, Bob needed to get a referral from his doctor. He had to wait a month just to sit down for 10 minutes with the surgeon, whose qualifications my acquaintance had to take primarily on faith. There was little to go on. No advertising. No fee schedules. No patient testimonials. Information necessary to make an informed decision was simply not accessible.

What would be the cost of hip replacement surgery? Even asking the question seemed subversive. He wanted to know about outcomes. How quickly did the surgeon's other patients return to work? What was their experience with mobility, pain, and functional capacity? How did the postoperative experience of this particular surgeon's patients differ from the experience of other surgeons? And how many hip replacement surgeries had the surgeon conducted? What was the infection rate at the selected hospital compared to other hospitals? And, because costs are never far from Bob's mind, all things being equal, could he get a better outcome for less money someplace else?

I'm happy to report that the surgery went very well and I occasionally see Bob on the tennis court. Although he still doesn't know the final cost for his new hip, he still considers it outrageous—and this from someone who buys and sells billion-dollar companies. When he was discharged from the hospital, Bob received lengthy itemized bills from the hospital, the surgeon, the anesthesiologist, and other members of the healthcare team. What really galls him is that he couldn't discover the price prior to buying and he couldn't understand the charges after the purchase was made.

Now consider the experience of a second acquaintance who decided to go to another type of surgeon for another type of procedure.

Ever since he was an adolescent, Dave was self-conscious about his nose and finally decided to consult a cosmetic surgeon about getting a rhinoplasty—commonly called a nose job. Today a VP-level sales executive, Dave was also determined to do research and make an informed buying decision.

Dave's experience could not have been more different from Bob's. All the cosmetic surgeons were happy to meet and discuss prices and outcomes. Dave was called a "client" not a "patient" and his needs came first. Each doctor willingly quoted package prices so that he could easily make comparisons. Web sites discussed the doctor's credentials and expected outcomes. Some sites not only displayed actual before-and-after photographs of rhinoplasties, but offered an animation feature that allowed him to superimpose different noses on images of his face. Surgeons offered the names and phone numbers of satisfied patients who agreed to be contacted as references. The doctors tried to outdo themselves in customer service. Some offered to send a limousine to pick Dave up. They all provided a variety of payment options. Dave made a decision, and two weeks later he had the surgery. Moreover, he knows to the penny what his new nose cost.

What accounts for the difference between the nose job and the hip replacement surgeries?

Competition. It works when we let it. If you check the price history of rhinoplasty with that of hip replacements, the power of competition to lower costs is undeniable. On average, the real cost of rhinoplasty has come down. The price of hip replacement surgery has inflated at the same rate as that of healthcare, about twice that of the economy in general. What's the difference?

Cosmetic surgeons have to compete directly for clients who pay for services out of their pockets. Because orthopedic surgeons serve patients who are referred by primary physicians, it is to the referring physician that specialists are most beholden. There is very little incentive for surgeons to be responsive to patients. And because the bills go to an insurance company, there is very little incentive for anyone to care about costs. That's the main difference. It's not a perfect system—I'd like to see even more quality data—but the cosmetic surgery sector works the way markets are supposed to work.

Again, I don't want to be accused of blaming anyone. It's not that cosmetic surgeons are smarter or more caring than orthopedic surgeons. If I'm in a car wreck, I'm probably going to be grateful to both of these skilled professionals. Both do the best they can within the confines of the incentives we provide. It's the incentives—and the levels at which the incentives come into play—that need adjusting.

It really boils down to who pays. Because health insurance rarely covers cosmetic surgery, people who want cosmetic surgery have to pay for it out-of-pocket. When people spend their own hard-earned money, they are much more conscious about costs and outcomes. Cosmetic surgeons must therefore appeal directly to consumers primarily on the basis of value—quality and price. The industry responds with innovation that results in better outcomes, lower prices, and a higher level of customer satisfaction.

By contrast, the executive who had hip surgery was insured. As we have noted, third-party payments create an incentive structure that makes high cost inevitable. Yes, the executive's health insurance company totally paid for his procedure. But the cost included loss of control. He was told which doctor to see and had little control and less information on which to evaluate the value he received.

It's worth noting that no one mandated that the cosmetic surgery industry provide this level of innovation. Government bureaucrats didn't write specifications requiring such innovation. Insurance companies didn't make them do it. There was no law mandating that cosmetic surgeons post their fees. Individual cosmetic surgeons figured all this out because it was in their self-interest to do so. When competition is working well, efficiencies usually arise on the supply side. These innovations tend to be effective because providers decide the best way to deliver it.

One of the big problems with managed care is that it attempts to impose an outcome from the top down by dictate, and then directs healthcare professionals how to do it. This type of innovation frequently fails to deliver its intended benefits. It's one thing to challenge doctors to figure out how to do something more efficiently. It's another to tell them how to do it.

If medicine worked like other markets, every doctor would be interested in learning what Johns Hopkins perfected about outpatient mastectomy surgery. It's not easy for doctors to embrace best practices because there are few incentives for them to perform more innovative medicine or to measure their performance relative to other doctors. The pace of adoption of new practices in medicine is slower than in any other industry. If, right now, we suddenly had the answers to the system's problems patented and ready to go, they wouldn't be widely implemented in the lifetimes of many readers of this book. The reality is that the system simply does not provide physicians with strong incentives to practice innovative medicine. Cost-containment, not innovation, characterizes medicine today.

Zero-Sum Competition

Management, such as it is, of the healthcare system has evolved into a zero-sum game. As participants in the system fight over costs, they end up dividing healthcare value instead of increasing it. This is the essence of zero-sum competition: an assumption that we have to battle over limited resources and that one party's gain comes only at the expense of another. Zero-sum competition bespeaks a narrow, stunted view of community and human aspirations. It's the mantra of the selfish. We recognize it in the punch line of jokes:[1]

Person Number 1: I have a job interview today. Wish me luck.

Person Number 2: No. If you get extra luck, there might be less available for me.

The joke is funny because zero-sum competition is rarely stated so directly. What's not funny is the attitude of cynicism embedded deeply in healthcare economics. There it degrades value by its exclusive insistence that costs alone be the overriding concern of participants in the healthcare system. As participants consider increasingly narrow slices of cost, they actually erode value by encouraging duplication and imposing unnecessary administrative overhead. I believe the emphasis on costs—containing them, avoiding them, shifting them—has crowded out real opportunities for competition to drive up value for patients.

Fortunately, zero-sum competition can be replaced throughout the healthcare value chain by what I call "value-added" competition. Under value-added competition, all restrictions on choice at the disease or treatment level disappear, including preapprovals for referrals. Information on treatments, alternatives, and providers' experience would be made available to consumers to enable comparison-shopping. Pricing for treatments would be transparent and billing would be simplified. Healthcare providers would have to work harder under this approach, but consumers would receive more value for their healthcare investments.

There is a simple test to determine if a course of action supports zero-sum or value-added competition, suggests Michael Porter in his influential *Harvard Business Review* article, "Redefining Competition in Healthcare."[2] If the question driving the course of action asks, "Who pays?" it is zero-sum competition. If the question driving the course of action asks, "Who provides the best value?" it is value-added competition. "It is at this level that true value is created—or destroyed—disease by disease, patient by patient," Porter says. Many of the insights noted in this chapter are drawn from Michael Porter's work.

For the healthcare industry to actually receive the benefits of competition, we must eliminate all activities that take the form of cost shifting. Passing costs from the payer to the patient, from the insurance company to the hospital, from the hospital to the physician, from the insured to the uninsured, creates no net value. If we continue on this course, the U.S. healthcare industry, representing one-fifth of the entire economy, becomes little more than a giant game of "hot potato." When gains for one participant come at the expense of another, we are playing a zero-sum game. In such a contest, the party with the least power—unfortunately, the patient—always ends up holding the hot potato.

Ultimately, a healthcare system creates value only at the moment of truth when the patient meets the doctor. Other healthcare activities, important as they are, exist to support this interaction. The pharmaceutical industry, for instance, creates value by working hard to develop new medicines. But we add value only when a physician prescribes the medicine and, as a consequence, the patient benefits.

Everything else is overhead. It might be critical, but activities such as doctor training, hospital administration, patient lab work, and pharmaceutical R&D are supported by the value created when patients and physicians work together to increase the net store of health in the world.

When the emphasis moves away from cost shifting and settles on prevention and early intervention, healthcare actually expands wealth and creates more opportunities for everyone. Today, with the exception of the cosmetic surgery industry, the eye care industry, and some dentistry, there is little significant competition at the disease and symptom level. We need much more competition at the disease and symptom level, the point at which the healthcare system creates value in the form of prevention, diagnosis, and treatment.

Competition of Victims

What little competition there is in the healthcare system creates more harm than good because it sets up participants to be victims. Healthcare is as contentious as it is because every participant clamors to have their victimization be enshrined as the most noble.

Doctors feel victimized by personal injury lawyers, health plans feel victimized by government payers, patients feel victimized by the pharmaceutical industry, and employees feel victimized by health plans. Any system organized around which participant is the greater victim must be detrimental to the health of every party involved.

One of the major problems with zero-sum competition is that in breeding victims it also nourishes an adversarial climate. The result is that when it comes time to settle disputes, there is little alternative but to involve the legal system, the most costly form of conflict resolution. Injecting lawyers or the threat of malpractice lawsuits into healthcare only increases costs and anxiety. The legal fees incurred by doctors and the malpractice insurance premiums they are forced to pay distort healthcare. But these costs, as significant as they are, are dwarfed by the indirect costs generated by doctors practicing unnecessary, defensive medicine.

Value-Added Competition

Value-added competition occurs at the level of preventing, identifying, and treating patients' conditions and diseases. It is at the patient and symptom level where huge differences in cost and quality persist. It is at the doctor's office where patients decide if they are satisfied with the value they have received for their investment. And it is at the outcome level where measurement is most meaningful. Nowhere else will competition find better traction in trimming costs, improving efficiency and effectiveness, reducing errors, and sparking innovation. Competition at the level of individual patients and health conditions is all but totally missing.[3]

Now consider quality of choice and information under a value-added competition model. When competition is directly connected to health-care value, providers compete for patients on a symptom or disease level. Suppose that you and your primary physician determine that it's time you received a hip replacement. Under a system of value-added competition, you would see increased specialization by healthcare providers. Thousands of doctors and clinics specializing in hip replacements would compete for your business on the basis of who could do the best job, with the fewest complications, and the best recovery records. Pricing and statistical information about outcomes would be readily available so you could make intelligent comparisons and actionable decisions. Based on these factors, the clinic you select might well be outside your state or even the country.

Shifting from zero-sum to value-added competition will not be easy. It will require changes in the infrastructure of the healthcare industry, a redesign of the business models of healthcare providers, and change in the behavior of employers purchasing health plans. I envision a transition period in which both the current and new healthcare systems will exist side-by-side.

I'm confident that the infrastructure changes can be made. There's reason to believe that healthcare providers are willing to consider changes to failing business models. As for the behavior of employers, I lead an organization of 115,000 people, and I am on the record as favoring transformation in this area. I know many CEOs who also think the status quo is unfair and unsustainable; they would welcome being freed of the responsibility for the healthcare of their employees so they can focus on creating value for the customers.

Here are five areas of the *status quo* that we will need to change to create the right incentives for value-added competition:

1. Specialization
2. Price transparency
3. Simplified billing
4. Free flow of information
5. Increasing the supply of healthcare professionals

Let's look at each one in turn.

Specialization

We've long known that real economies result from specialization. Simplicity and repetition breed competence. Modern firms outsource all but their most mission-central activities because they welcome the benefits of partnering with someone who can perform a particular activity more efficiently. We see this in every corner of our economy as healthcare providers stake out increasingly narrow slices of the value chain.

When my son's car needs an oil change, he takes it to one of those specialty franchises that do nothing but oil changes and lube jobs. Now that Jamie's Jeep is in their database, it's amazing how quickly and inexpensively they can service his car. But we really shouldn't be surprised. That's all they do—and they do it hundreds of times a day.

Sears, Roebuck and Co., which operates general automobile service centers, got the same message. Sears selected Jiffy Lube, a quick oil change chain, to provide this service at many of its car care centers, because, as a Sears spokesman notes, "we could not do oil changes in as focused and professional a way as can Jiffy Lube."[4] Yet when it comes to medical care, although practitioners may recognize the benefits of specialization, most do not follow through because of the structural impediments of the healthcare system.

To align with the precepts of value-added healthcare, doctors should reorganize around practice areas. Instead of trying to be all things to all people, value-added competitors think about practice areas that need innovation and zero in. Real value is created when providers create distinctive value, either in the complexity of conditions they treat, or in subgroups of patients they have become uniquely good at engaging. The goal is to migrate services in a direction in which they are most needed. No longer can we afford to tie up expensive space on medical campuses with services that can be provided more cheaply elsewhere.

Everyone wins if healthcare providers focus on adding as much value as they can at the patient and symptom level. Frequently, that will mean specializing in one symptom, disease, or therapy.

There are plenty of examples that show the power of specialization at the symptom level. For example, if I ever need a hernia repair, my first call would be to Shouldice Hospital, a clinic near Toronto, Canada that has achieved extraordinary results in hernia surgery. The Shouldice example touches on so many elements of value-added competition in healthcare that it deserves a closer look.

A hernia occurs when a weakness in the abdominal wall allows a loop of intestine to push through. In most hospitals or surgery centers, hernia repairs are done on an outpatient basis by surgeons whose practice usually includes other surgical procedures. The surgery itself takes about 90 minutes. The average cost in the United States is about $5000, in part because of liability expenses. Moreover, for about one patient in eight, the hernia returns, according to the Hernia Society of America. In the United States, it is nearly impossible for patients to determine the failure rate of individual surgeons performing hernia repairs.

None of these facts apply at the 89-bed Shouldice facility, which handles hernias and nothing else, over 275,000 and counting. At Shouldice, hernia operations take 30-45 minutes. And even though the Shouldice treatment includes four days of hospitalization, the costs are about $2500. The dozen surgeons at Shouldice do hernia operations and nothing else. The recurrence rate for hernia procedures at Shouldice is just 1 percent, compared to an average failure rate of about 12 percent at general hospitals.

Shouldice is ferocious about collecting statistics on its performance, and its surgeons do not shy away from accountability. Surgeons who operate on a patient whose hernia recurs must provide the surgery again, at no charge. Each January, as part of a lifetime follow-up, the clinic invites former patients for a reunion in Toronto where doctors check outcomes. Patients who cannot make it in person are asked to fill out detailed questionnaires. Shouldice has used the results to compile the world's most extensive statistics on hernia repair.

The entire facility is designed around the specific health needs of hernia patients. The surgeons know that physical activity helps prevent problems associated with inactivity, such as pneumonia or blood clots, and also promotes quicker healing of the abdominal wall. For that reason, rooms have no telephones or televisions. Patients have to walk to a lounge to make a phone call or watch TV. Meals are served downstairs in the cafeteria and patients are encouraged to use the stairs. A recreation room features a pool table to promote stretching. Outside, patients will find a putting green to encourage bending as well as walking paths to encourage strolling.

By its focus on specialization, technology, rigorous reporting, and emphasis on customer outcomes, Shouldice is practicing value-added competition. Although it has identified best practices for hernia repair, it is always searching for incremental improvements it can incorporate across its practice.

Healthcare providers in the United States and elsewhere who want to replicate Shouldice's success must understand that while a clear focus on one procedure or medical condition is essential, specialization by itself is no guarantee of anything. Success flows from a coordinated approach to everything that supports the specialization. "The thousands of details in Shouldice's integrated operating system—details of recruiting, training, compensation, facility design, and process engineering— provide the key," says Regina Herzlinger, author of *Market Driven Health Care: Who Wins, Who Loses in the Transformation of America's Largest Service Industry*. "These thousands of details would be difficult to replicate in a setting that has a broader set of objectives."[5]

Recently, health insurance companies are trying to improve clinical outcomes and lower costs by identifying and harnessing the healthcare professionals who are "best of breed" in their specialties. Aetna, for instance, offers employees and clients a program that features a network of specialists who have shown that they adhere to best-practices guidelines. Specialists are included in the program if they demonstrate good clinical performance and cost-efficiency across such areas as hospital readmission rates, adverse events, and specialty-specific measures.

Aetna uses a four-step process to determine who will be in the network. First, a specialist must have at least 10 "episodes of care" in the Aetna database. Then the plan looks at clinical quality indicators. These might include a physician's 30-day readmission rate and his complication rate for hospitalized patients. Specialty-specific measures rely on how well the doctor's care conforms to specialty medical society guidelines. For cardiologists, for example, Aetna considers how many patients with cardiac disease are taking lipid-lowering drugs, and how many patients with congestive heart failure are on ACE inhibitors. The program covers 12 specialties, ranging from general surgery to specialties such as OB/GYN, neurosurgery, and orthopedics.

If employees choose the doctors deemed most skilled and cost-conscious, they pocket rewards: a reduction in their copayment or co-insurance, or a reduction in their deductible. The physician gets no additional pay, only the opportunity to attract more patients.

Centers of Specialization

Centers of specialization are springing up all over the world, signaling a global market for healthcare. People in Europe have long sought healthcare in neighboring countries. Increasingly, medical clinics in developing countries are attracting Americans with focused healthcare needs.

The Escorts Heart Institute & Research Centre in New Delhi, India, is an example of this trend. Escorts specializes in replacing damaged human heart valves with valves harvested from pigs, and promotes itself on the basis of price as well as quality. It seems to have a good case on both levels. The total bill at Escorts for a heart valve replacement is about $10,000, including round-trip airfare from the United States and a side trip to the Taj Mahal. A similar procedure in the United States would run in the neighborhood of $200,000. For an American patient who needs a new heart valve but has no health insurance, Indian clinics look increasingly attractive.

India is working feverishly to establish a reputation for excellence in healthcare. The country has a long way to go in upgrading the health systems for its millions of impoverished citizens. Yet for the clinics serving foreign visitors, the quality of care is as good as or better than that of big-city hospitals in the United States or Europe. For example, the death rate for coronary-bypass patients at Escorts is 0.8 percent. By contrast, the 1999 death rate for the same procedure at New York-Presbyterian Hospital, where former President Bill Clinton underwent heart bypass surgery, was 2.35 percent, according to a 2002 study by the New York State Health Department.[6]

The phenomenon is another example of how India is profiting from globalization—the growing integration of world economies—just as it has in such other service industries as insurance and banking, which are outsourcing a growing assortment of office tasks to the country. A recent study by the McKinsey consulting firm estimated India's medical-tourist industry could yield up to $2.2 billion in annual revenue by 2012.[7]

I believe increased competition through globalization will have at least two positive results. Within India, and nations like Singapore, wishing to capitalize on the search for medical value, the practices developed by clinics to serve foreign visitors will migrate to clinics serving the general population. Outside of these nations, global competition will add one more dimension to the forces exerting a downward pressure on healthcare costs. More fundamentally, if the centers of one nation develop better clinical procedures, we can hope that clinics elsewhere in the world will sit up and take notice. Who knows, perhaps a cardiovascular clinic in Buffalo will start throwing in a side trip to Niagara Falls.

Price Transparency

Healthcare is complicated and highly personalized, so it's probably not possible for doctors to post prices like service stations do: so much for a tire rotation, so much for a tune-up. But customized software applications are also complicated and highly personalized, and yet prices can be quoted in advance. Doctors and hospitals can do a lot better posting the prices for various services. By doing so, they can begin to give patients meaningful price estimates.

Posting prices offers two main benefits. First, the practice creates a price consciousness among both patients and providers that, in the long run, exerts a constraint on consumption and a downward pressure on costs. Only when both patients and providers know the cost of a proposed test or procedure can they consider if it's truly cost-effective. Only providers who learn about their costs have a chance of reducing or eliminating them.

But the second benefit might be even more significant. Posting prices tends to standardize prices. This is important because right now, providers charge vastly different prices to different group affiliations for addressing the same medical condition. I want to encourage a tight link between the fees a provider charges and the provider's actual costs. It is another form of cost shifting for providers to charge one fee just because Patient A is insured by Blue Cross and a different fee because Patient B is covered by Cigna.

The outcome is discriminatory in that some people have their health needs covered, while those who are unemployed or whose employers do not cover them have to pay artificially high list prices. In effect, patients covered by the largest groups are subsidized by members of smaller groups and the uninsured and out-of-network patients who pay list prices. All this does is make health insurance more expensive, further adding to the ranks of people who cannot afford health insurance which, in turn, increases the uncompensated care expenses of hospitals.

By advocating price transparency, I am definitely not advocating price controls. Ideally, I want to see robust competition among providers in the prices they set, but that pricing would reflect the cost to all patients, not just the networks who manage to negotiate the best discounts. I'd expect health insurance groups to negotiate for the best rates based on volume. All others could shop for the best arrangement.

Automobile service stations are free to set their prices to whatever they like. But competition and price transparency tends to bunch prices for any given service in a tight zone around a median. Whatever that price is, service stations charge the same price for everyone.

Simplified Billing

As Bob with the new hip can attest, current healthcare billing practices are frustrating and confusing. The confusion results from the system's refusal to hold itself accountable. The function of pricing is to convey information to consumers and competitors, and yet healthcare invoices make price and value comparisons virtually impossible. When every provider submits a separate invoice for each separate service, billing practices become just another form of cost shifting.

I believe we can do better. Under value-added competition, each provider would have to issue a single invoice for each treatment cycle. Ideally, agreements among healthcare providers would allow patients to receive an integrated invoice that covers all the services performed on his or her behalf in the course of the treatment cycle. "Many other industries have solved the problem of how to issue a single bill for customized services; among them aerospace construction, auto repair, and professional services consulting," Prof. Porter notes. "A competitive healthcare industry could figure it out too."[8]

Free Flow of Information

Value-added competition is not possible unless lubricated by the free flow of information that today is considered confidential, proprietary, or embarrassing. Without such information, neither providers nor consumers can make intelligent decisions about health and costs. Here the disclosure of healthcare information I am calling for is akin to the disclosure about corporate financial matters overseen by the SEC or the disclosure of pharmaceutical clinical trials overseen by the FDA. More disclosure, rather than less, will unleash the power of competition to eliminate waste and encourage lower prices, more innovation, and better outcomes.

At a minimum, we would see healthcare providers post pricing information for specific healthcare services. Consumers would use pricing information to make cost-sensitive decisions and to hold the providers accountable. Another set of data would collect information about the risk-adjusted medical outcomes that the patients of specific healthcare providers have experienced. This is not unlike the service repair data that *Consumer Reports* lists for specific makes of automobiles. Here, the information would be specific to particular diseases, treatments, or medical conditions. If you were considering entrusting Physician A with your hip replacement or angioplasty, wouldn't you like to know his or her track record in terms of functional recovery times, complications, and even the disposition of medical malpractice lawsuits?

In the present legal climate, we can expect physicians to oppose disseminating information that will make them more accountable. Physicians are acting rationally when they resist programs that generate information that will probably be used against them in court. This is a big problem that will require significant healthcare liability reform to address. But we don't have to wait for tort reform to start disseminating information about health outcomes. When public safety is at stake, we have precedents for collecting the needed information despite the objections of powerful groups that are threatened by its collection.

It has not been widely publicized, for example, but many late-model automobiles have a safety feature that is triggered by the deployment of air bags. This safety feature works like the "black boxes" on airplanes that Federal Aviation Agency analysts can study to determine the cause of an airplane accident. In the case of automobiles, this black box records such information as the speed of the car on impact, whether the driver applied the brakes, and whether the driver was wearing safety belts at time of impact. The information collected helps engineers improve car passenger safety by determining whether the air-bag systems were effective as designed. This is the important goal for collecting this information.

By law, the black box data is strictly for the use of safety engineers. That's the key point. Although the data recovered from individual black boxes in the case of individual accidents might be of interest both to law enforcement officials—who want it to reconstruct the accident—and personal injury lawyers—who want it to fix liability—the information is generally denied them. Law enforcement officials need a court order signed by a judge to obtain the data. Personal injury lawyers and other private individuals cannot get access to the data under any circumstances.

Until meaningful medical malpractice reform is underway, we cannot build the databases that can give patients the information they need to make decisions about selecting individual physicians. The information in such databases will, no doubt, be of interest to personal injury lawyers, but safeguards can be put in place to protect physicians. Most lawyers already have access to the information likely to be aggregated in such databases. The only parties left in the dark are the individual patients, who have the most to gain by making informed decisions.

Increasing the Supply of Healthcare Professionals

Some of my physician friends will not like my saying this, but another way to increase competition in healthcare is to allow trained healthcare professionals such as paramedics, nurses, and physician's assistants to do some of the jobs that are now by law restricted to medical doctors. This solution could satisfy both the needs of patients for more access to healthcare and the need to keep healthcare costs down.

I am not alone in raising the argument that one reason that healthcare is too costly or inaccessible in some areas is that we insist on delivering so much of it through highly trained physicians. Nurses, nurse-practitioners, and physician's assistants could do a lot of what we now rely on doctors to do—and they could do it at a lower cost. They could also expand access to medical care in poor and rural areas.

A pediatrician with a practice in St. Louis recently complained to me that she had just been awakened four times in one night by patients with concerns about their children's health. I commiserated with her. My job has its difficulties, but at least I am not routinely called in the middle of the night by distraught shareholders. And then I asked a question. "How many of those patient calls did your nurses have the training and experience to handle?" The pediatrician thought for a minute and responded, "All of them."

Medicine is one of the most tightly regulated sectors in the entire economy. The stated purpose of the regulations is to protect patients, but the regulations also have the effect of raising entry barriers to the profession, limiting supply, raising fees, and depriving patients of options they might happily choose. Licensing of physicians in the United States arose in the nineteenth century mainly as a way of limiting the supply of doctors and thus shielding the profession from competition.

Privately, most physicians will concede that trained paraprofessionals are capable of providing many of the routine services that are restricted to licensed doctors. Does it really promote public safety to require doctors to perform tasks that paraprofessionals can do just as safely? Wouldn't it make sense to delegate as many services as possible to lower-cost, trained medical assistants and reserve for physicians the most skill-intensive procedures?

The rural clinics of sub-Saharan Africa couldn't operate any other way. A shortage of physicians has created the opportunity for medical paraprofessionals to diagnose and treat major killers such as malaria, tuberculosis, and pneumonia. These health workers perform hundreds of thousands of lifesaving treatments and even minor surgeries. Results have been very positive. What the paraprofessionals might lack in formal training, they make up for in repetition.

International health experts say that these paraprofessionals offer a solution to two of the most vexing problems confronting African countries. First, Africa's medical schools can't graduate physicians fast enough to deal with the catastrophic epidemics of disease facing the continent. Even if they could, the brain drain of African physicians to European countries with doctor shortages of their own would ensure that most of Africa's rural clinics remain doctorless. It's a double-whammy crisis that only paraprofessional systems can address.

Countries such as Malawi, whose sole medical school is just a dozen years old and has produced only 206 doctors, is the victim of a devastating exodus of nurses and midwives to the United Kingdom.[9] The physician brain drain in developing countries such as Malawi is the flip side of relentless cost-shifting policies in Western countries that replace higher-cost Western doctors with lower-cost African doctors.

Paraprofessionals—known as "clinical officers" in Malawi; "technicos" in Mozambique, and as "surgical technicians" throughout Africa—now outnumber doctors three-to-one in the public health system. They represent the front line of African public health response to AIDS care as the continent begins a long-awaited expansion of drug treatment.

Medical school and the brutality of the multiyear training regimen for physicians is defended as a Darwinian process that selects the most outstanding individuals to be doctors. I have watched my own son navigate this ordeal, and I am convinced there is a better way to train young physicians, but that discussion will take us far afield from my two main points. First, that the current selection process unnecessarily deters many quality people from going into medicine by virtue of its harshness and cost. Second, that medical regulations limit the types of treatment that other health professionals, such as physician's assistants and nurse-midwives, could provide at much lower cost without serious compromise to patient safety.

Complete Triumph of Competition

In 1991, the Soviet Union collapsed, signaling the triumph of societies disciplined by decentralized, customer-driven, and free-market economies—overcentralized, price-controlled, and command-and-control-driven economies.

Leaders in the United States never hesitate to lecture other peoples of the world to embrace these principles. Yet when it comes to America's healthcare system, we fail to heed our own advice. Most of the ills of our present healthcare system can be remedied if we simply accept for ourselves the recommendations we advocate for others.

I can assure you that, despite the very real risks, I would much prefer to be exposed to the full force of market competition than to overbroad government regulation. There is need for regulation, and I welcome much of it, but we must acknowledge that while specific regulations are generally adopted in good faith and often have positive benefits, they always impose costs and frequently trigger the law of unintended consequences.

Societies place differing values on competition. American culture, which places a high value on competition, also tolerates a high level of inequality. Other societies, which place a high value on equality of outcomes, tend to substitute centralized regulation for competitive activity. The question I am left with is this: In the face of growing international competition, what is the best way for each nation to order its priorities and to allocate the energies of its most talented citizens to the tasks at hand? History has demonstrated that for all its problems, competition is the best way to steer the most productive workers to the most productive enterprises. Allocation of resources cannot be predetermined. If the economic collapse of the Communist Bloc countries can be traced to a single factor, it is their dismal performance in allocating resources. The challenge of competitive societies is to narrow the resulting inequalities so that every participant benefits from a level playing field and has a stake in the system.

My final point is that positive-sum competition in healthcare is good for everyone, including the poor and the uninsured. It's easy for critics of competition and accountability to accuse people who favor markets of not caring for the poor. My position is that competition and related healthcare reforms in the world's healthcare systems will generate enough health, productivity, and savings to cover everyone, regardless of their ability to pay.

Let me be clear about this so there is no mistaking my position: Markets do create winners and losers. But it is in society's interest that everyone has a positive stake in the healthcare system, regardless of ability to pay.

Eliminating zero-sum competition will not be easy because cost-shifting, once experienced, is terribly seductive. Bold leadership will be needed to overcome the resistance of vested interests who have grown powerful under this system. Regulated, free-market competition is a powerful force for social betterment. It offers the best hope for delivering market discipline in the form of cost reductions, higher quality, "take-your-breath-away innovation," and fewer medical errors.

CHAPTER 8

HEALTH CREATES WEALTH: NO ONE LEFT BEHIND

A mong the developed countries of the world, the United States alone tolerates a level of inequality that puts adequate healthcare beyond the reach of millions of its citizens. Our nation's leaders lament this situation, but have not been able to articulate a solution. We seem to be constrained by the difficulties of raising funds to pay for the presumably budget-breaking solution to the problem of the uninsured. My goal is to reframe the issue of healthcare access in a way that might suggest new solutions. While this chapter focuses on the situation in the United States, I believe many of the issues apply in general terms to the healthcare systems of other nations.

As a society, Americans have not been able to get traction on this problem because of three misconceptions. Let me speak about these briefly, and we'll come back to each for a more detailed discussion.

We are, first, worried about something that is a misnomer. What we call "health insurance" is not really *insurance* as most of us know it. It's about sickness, not health. If we want health insurance for all, we need to be more precise about what that means.

Second, we assume that the lack of health insurance for all is a problem of the uninsured. It's not. It's a problem for the insured that has dire consequences for the poor and uninsured.

We are, third, limiting our options by assuming that making health insurance available to Americans who need it, and who are not currently insured, will require a massive injection of new funds. Not so. All the money needed is already being spent.

I realize that these are bold statements, so let me try to get clarity around these three misconceptions and help spark new thinking on alternative solutions.

Why Do We Call It Health Insurance?

Our language has confused us. What we mean by *health* insurance is actually *sickness* insurance. By whatever term, it operates more as *prepayment* for inevitable sickness expenses rather than insurance to reimburse us for occasional sickness expenses. One of the reasons healthcare costs are rising uncontrollably is because we are trying to control the wrong things.

We see the same confusion built into other insurance products. For example, life insurance is really death insurance. Of course, trying to get people to buy something called "death insurance" is a nonstarter, so the insurance industry made the name more positive. "Life insurance" is an understandable marketing euphemism that has no significant negative consequences to society. Most of us understand that when we buy life insurance, death is what we insure. To make informed decisions, we need to accept that the "life" the policy insures is that of the beneficiary.

Less benign are the consequences of mistaking *health* insurance for *sickness* insurance. When we pay for sickness insurance, sickness—and the infrastructure to treat it—is what we get. Pretending that we are buying health insurance when, in reality, we are paying for sickness accounts for much of the frustration about healthcare costs that we now face.

Healthcare insurance has drifted far away from what most people think of as insurance. Perhaps a story will illustrate what I mean by healthcare insurance not behaving like other insurance products. Some years ago, a large tree branch fell on my house. Thankfully, no one was hurt, but the house sustained some damage. I had a property hazard policy in force, and after getting an estimate from a carpenter, the insurance company sent me a check to cover the repairs, less my deductible.

This is true insurance, an arrangement by which a company gives customers financial protection against loss or harm. In exchange for a premium I paid up-front, the insurance company agreed to assume the financial risk of an unlikely accident. The events the company insured me against are defined as rare, significant, and occurring by chance—certainly not under the control of the insured.

Healthcare is not like insuring a home against damage. You probably know people who have never made a claim on their property hazard insurance policy and are glad of it. Contrast this with so-called healthcare insurance. The reality about health insurance is that everyone gets sick from time to time, and as we get older we tend to get sick more often. Do you know anyone who has never been sick? Do we not look to health insurance to reimburse us for routine illness? Benjamin Franklin reminds us that nothing in life is more certain than death and taxes. To that list, I believe we can add the certainty of claims against every health insurance policy.

When a car accident occurs, the resulting expenses often represent a profound setback to one's financial standing. It is to hedge the risk of that kind of setback that we buy automobile liability insurance. But when we get sick, the expenses we want reimbursed—a visit to the doctor, the cost of a blood test, a prescription medicine—are not always significant. True insurance is supposed to protect people against losses from rare high-cost events. Yet health insurance today covers routine expenses that are entirely under the patient's control. It is often the equivalent of auto insurance that covers fill-ups and oil changes. Today's health insurance is less *insurance* than *prepayment* of medical services.

When a car crash occurs, it usually happens by accident. It's often out of our control. But most of us have significant control over our health. Given what we know about the role of personal behavior—exercise, nutrition, smoking, etc.—to our health, most of us accept that to a greater or lesser degree some of the illnesses we face are as much under our control as by chance. The element of control in our health represents another difference between health insurance and other forms of insurance. Healthcare costs are rising more rapidly than necessary because we insist on treating healthcare events as the products of chance rather than what they are—predictable, inevitable, and even intentional actions.

Almost everyone buys insurance of some form or another. Some policies are optional (life insurance, mortgage insurance, theft insurance); other policies are mandated (automobile liability insurance, if you own a car); property hazard insurance (if you have a mortgage on your residence); medical malpractice insurance (if you want to practice medicine). The private market offers consumers a robust marketplace for all of these insurance products. Yet we do not look to our employers to purchase any of these for us.[1]

Other People's Money

Most healthcare systems alienate people from the medical insurance premiums paid to cover their health. In the United States, which delivers medical insurance primarily through employers, employees feel they are spending someone else's money when they consume healthcare services. Of course, the money they spend is their own, but the reality of third-party payments makes unnecessary spending inevitable.

In Chapter 3, we saw that an employee healthcare insurance policy is funded when an employer takes a portion of what an employee earns and uses it to pay the premium. Some employees might prefer that their employer add that sum to their paycheck, and trust them to handle their own healthcare needs, but under American tax policies that option is rarely available, nor is it financially advisable. The result is a sense on the part of most people that they have prepaid for unlimited health services, and unlimited health services are what they expect.

The Insured Own the Problem

As long as we persist in framing the issue of universal access as a problem of the uninsured, we're not going to get very far. The motivation to solve problems on behalf of others is never as powerful as the motivation to solve problems that are truly our own. The insured must own the problem if we are to move forward because it is insured people who have the most to lose. But how is this accomplished?

Let's start by acknowledging that insurance or no insurance, Americans who require medical care generally receive it. We are not a society willing to turn critically ill people away from hospitals. Medical insurance is less about guaranteeing access to health care than protecting one's financial assets against the costs of a catastrophic health crisis. But here's the key point about costs: the healthcare uninsured people typically consume is provided in hospital emergency rooms, the single most expensive way our system delivers services.

But that doesn't mean the services remain unpaid. Hospitals are businesses with their own bills to pay. We call services to the uninsured "uncompensated care" but that's just another misnomer. Just because the uninsured don't pay for it, that doesn't mean no one pays for it. Hospitals offset the costs incurred by uninsured patients by charging more to those who can pay. In practice, this means that costs across the board go up for public and private health insurance companies that pay the bills on behalf of the insured. These extra charges are passed along to the insured in the form of higher premiums, fees, and taxes.

Let's also acknowledge another unpleasant fact. The flip side of many Americans being underinsured is that many Americans are *overinsured*. These are people with health benefits provided by large employers or government programs. Some of these plans require only small copayments for doctor visits and other services. Others require payment of a deductible, after which the patient pays a portion of healthcare costs, such as 20 percent, up to some limit.

Under the American system, only the employer's spending on healthcare is fully tax-deductible. Furthermore, none of the employer-provided benefit is included in the employee's taxable income. By contrast, the unemployed, self-employed people, and employees of small businesses that do not offer health insurance get no deduction at all when they try to purchase insurance on their own. A self-employed person has to pay $10 to buy $10 of healthcare benefits. For covered employees, a similar level of healthcare costs about seven dollars. The difference is a subsidy to higher-income Americans working for big companies, paid for by the uninsured and small business owners.

In other words, patients covered by one sector are subsidized by patients in another sector. Within the private sector, patients in large groups are subsidized by members of smaller groups that do not have the same negotiating clout. All this cross-subsidization does is increase administrative costs and artificially raise list prices for the uninsured, raising the cost of entry to the system and adding to the numbers of people unable to afford healthcare. For hospitals, the lack of a level playing field drives up uncompensated care expenses (the cost of treating uninsured patients), making healthcare more costly for everyone.

The firms enjoying the biggest discounts might think they have a bargain. But without rational pricing and service-by-service competition, costs will continue to rise while quality lags. "The cost of dysfunctional competition far outweighs any short-term advantages system participants get from price discrimination—even for those firms that get the biggest discounts," says Michael Porter.[2]

The irony is that this tax policy, part of a "temporary" inflation-fighting measure initiated 60 years ago, is still very much with us. That is the nature of government regulation; it often outlives its usefulness. This tax benefit has emerged as a major obstruction in the quest for parity between those who are covered by their employers and everyone else. It is one reason why any proposals to empower all individuals, employed or not, through such initiatives as Medical Savings Accounts are found wanting. The tax bias in favor of employer-provided health insurance is overwhelming. It is little wonder that employers and employees opt for the tax-favored benefit over the tax-discouraged. In Chapter 9, I discuss the benefits of giving individuals more control over their healthcare spending.

The Money Is Already Spent

Because the workers are already paying for their healthcare as well as that of the poor and uninsured, the question of whether or not the nation can afford to extend health insurance to everyone has already been answered. Without realizing it, we are doing just that—and along the way, we've built the most expensive healthcare system on the planet. But measured by such standards as longevity, infant mortality, and infection rates, we are not receiving a lot of value from our investment.

The costs for "uncompensated care" for the poor and uninsured have already been rung up. The difference is that many of the current payments are not being made by the government; they are made directly by the uninsured poor or indirectly and unacknowledged by those with insurance. Moving to a formal insurance program would expose these costs to the light of day where both their appropriation and destination can be publicly debated. As it is, the tax sleight of hand is another example of the healthcare system shifting costs from one pocket to a pocket with holes in it on the same pair of pants.

We can recapture some of that value by shifting the emphasis in three fundamental ways.

First, people should be able to choose their healthcare directly, on the basis of the price they have to pay out of their own pockets. As we have seen, in the doctor-patient relationship, basic pricing information has been missing.

Second, the third-party tax discrimination favoring employer-paid health insurance must give way to a level playing field that will encourage individuals to take more responsibility for their own healthcare.

Third, health insurance is not something that is improved by tightly linking it to employment. We must ultimately find a way to relieve employers of a burden that they neither desire nor execute very adeptly.

Wrong End of Telescope

Focusing only on the cost of care is looking at health through the wrong end of a telescope. We can no longer afford to treat healthcare as a zero-sum game, with patients competing for limited resources, a game marked by winners and losers. Instead of shifting costs, let's think about shifting incentives.

We want our healthcare system to improve our health, but we reimburse it for treating us when we are sick. We pay our healthcare system to deliver medical procedures, but consuming medical procedures does not necessarily lead to improved health. Let's turn the telescope around and examine the big sky of opportunity: health improvement. A more effective system would regard healthcare investment to be desired rather than as a cost to be avoided.

We invest in healthcare by emphasizing prevention, wellness, early detection, and early treatment. We start by changing the questions we ask. Instead of "How do we control the cost of care?" we ask "How do we lift the burden of disease?" Instead of weighing the value of health through the lens of cost, let's consider the value of life. Healthcare dollars should be thought of not simply as payments, but rather as investments that reduce the cost of disease and help create healthier, more productive lives.

By investing in health, we create wealth. The converse is also true. I have witnessed what the absence of investment in healthcare can do. In some nations, the absence of investment in health, particularly around HIV/AIDS, is wiping out the most productive members of society, killing people and destroying the means of creating wealth. People are so debilitated they can't work, and the infrastructure for creating value disintegrates. Human beings are the ultimate resource, but only if they are healthy.

Prevention and an emphasis on early intervention, diagnosis, and treatment are desirable not just from a humanitarian perspective. These approaches can literally pay for themselves by creating more economic value than the costs of the healthcare. A compelling case for this conclusion has been advanced by economists Kevin Murphy and Robert Topel from the University of Chicago's Graduate School of Business. They conclude that Americans would enjoy enormous benefits from even modest progress in fighting the major diseases.[3]

Murphy and Topol demonstrate that even small reductions in the American death rate from common killers such as cancer and heart disease could lead to trillions of dollars in added economic benefits. This is the power of prevention. According to their analysis, a 10 percent decrease in the death rate of Americans from just two major killers, cancer and cardiovascular disease, would translate into $10 trillion in added economic benefits for Americans living today. That's almost as much as the Gross Domestic Product of the United States and certainly more than enough to pay for any healthcare required to achieve that 10 percent reduction. Knowing what we now know about both of these killers, 10 percent reductions in their death rates is low-hanging fruit—worth trillions.

If we could achieve similar reductions in deaths from other major killers, such as HIV/AIDS, chronic liver disease, diseases linked with smoking and obesity, auto accidents, or suicides and homicides, Murphy and Topol estimate that the nation could benefit by as much as $17 trillion over the life spans of Americans living today. Again, these benefits are within reach if we would shift the emphasis to prevention, wellness, early diagnosis, and early intervention.

We're already seeing some of the economic benefits Murphy and Topol suggest in the extension of the lives of people with HIV. Before the advent of new medicines, a positive HIV test started the equivalent of a ticking time bomb. Now, in most cases, the result of HIV infections in developed countries can be managed, and the death rates in the United States have dropped by two-thirds. Younger or older, most of these HIV-positive individuals remain productive workers, earning incomes, paying taxes.

In the last 20 years, the pharmaceutical industry has developed a number of medicines that in many cases eliminate the need for surgery. For example, a few years ago, the only effective treatment for stomach ulcers was surgery. When was the last time you heard of anyone being operated on for stomach ulcers? Today, the overwhelming number of people who suffer from ulcers can live healthy lives and continue to be productive workers by taking medications. Do people feel the drugs are expensive? Possibly, but they avoid the much higher costs of surgery, and the very real risks of anesthesia and infection.

It's true that prescription-drug spending in the United States has grown in recent years. Much of this spending increase is associated with higher quality. Newer medicines are much more effective than older ones in treating the same medical condition. Thanks to research by Frank Lichtenberg of Columbia University, we know that the cost of extending life for one year using new drugs comes to $424. This is a small fraction of the economic value of a life-year, which, according to Lichtenberg, economists value at $150,000.[4] That's a useful number to have for macroeconomic purposes, but I can't assign a value to preserving the life of my loved ones, and I assume you would have the same difficulty with yours.

Antipsychotic medications for ailments such as schizophrenia are undoubtedly expensive, but they are much less expensive than warehousing people in institutions. With modern medicines, many people who would otherwise be institutionalized are now functioning in outpatient treatment settings or are independent. Lichtenberg shows that for every one dollar in new pharmaceutical cost, society is saving $7.17 in keeping people out of hospitals. That is an enviable record, but in another example of shortsightedness, third-party payers often resist paying for the medicines.

Meanwhile, patients who are unable to afford insurance often remain chronically ill and continue to crowd into emergency rooms, the most expensive way a patient can receive basic healthcare. The uninsured continue to go to emergency rooms because that's their only guaranteed access to the healthcare system. Who pays for these failures of our system? We all do.

Reducing congestion in hospital emergency rooms can mean the difference between life and death for people with serious medical situations. Emergency rooms are often terrific at delivering acute care, but far less proficient at delivering routine care, the kind of care the uninsured often seek at the ER.

A friend living in Florida—let's call him Dennis—told me the following story. One Saturday night, Dennis' wife complained of chest pains, difficulty breathing, and faintness— classic signs of a heart attack. Alarmed, Dennis immediately put his wife in the car and drove to the emergency room. He was amazed and then angered by the scene before him. It looked like the waiting room at the bus station. There was a long line of people waiting to be seen. He grew increasingly frustrated as he realized that the people between his wife and a doctor were dealing with mostly routine medical conditions. There were a couple of women with coughing infants. A man wanted to be seen for a bee sting. Another had a splinter. Meanwhile Dennis' wife was having a very hard time and the line wasn't moving. Dennis is very resourceful, so he stepped outside and dialed 911 to report an emergency. Within a minute, a stretcher was wheeled out and his wife was taken to see a doctor. Dennis told me he was shaken, not only by his wife's medical scare, but by his feelings of rage that the emergency room resource was being squandered.

Medically, things worked out well for Dennis' wife. An EKG showed she was having heart palpitations, not a heart attack. But Dennis emerged from the experience with a large bill for emergency room services and a sense of resentment against the emergency healthcare system. Timely medical care for his wife was threatened by large numbers of people forced to use the emergency room for routine medical care. This last-resort public health service for the under- and uninsured in our society is losing the confidence of those asked to fund it. Pitting the haves and the have-nots against each other is another destructive symptom of zero-sum competition in action.

A Framework for Health

Many of the diseases that force people into treatment and create costs within our healthcare system could be prevented. One way to do that is to adjust incentives. I believe that a national commitment to shift the focus of healthcare to the value of prevention, wellness, rapid diagnosis, and early treatment is the better choice for the future. As part of this shift, I am committed to shifting Pfizer's role. I want patients to see Pfizer as a partner in their efforts to stay well. To do that, Pfizer needs to occupy the health and wellness end of the continuum as much as the sick care end.

Changing the nation's focus will lead to a healthcare system that makes the most of America's best virtues—individual freedom, personal responsibility, and community caring. This new focus begins by envisioning a system that lowers the costs of disease—a system anchored in five "I" words: Inclusive, Individualized, Innovative, Information-Driven, and Incentives. We have spoken about some of these topics already, and the book devotes entire chapters to their benefits, but they have not formally been introduced. Let me remedy that right now.

Inclusive

America's healthcare system must include every American. Neither ability to pay nor quality of health must interfere with the ability of every American to participate in the system. Access must be the foundation for a new covenant in American healthcare. Improving access need not mean reducing standards of care.

At a minimum, the system I envision requires that no American should lack access to healthcare because he or she lacks the ability to pay for it, and that no American should suffer significant financial distress or personal bankruptcy as a result of unpaid medical bills. Within that definition, I can accommodate a broad spectrum of health insurance approaches with varying shades of individual financial protection.

The key point is that universal health insurance is not merely about solving the problem of the uninsured. Inclusiveness is good for everyone: insured and uninsured alike. Inclusiveness improves health, and better health leads to higher labor force participation and higher income. Inclusiveness should be pursued not only because of common decency, but because it supports a well-functioning market economy that lifts all boats. Uninsured people in poor health and lacking health insurance cannot be said to have equal opportunities in a market economy.

Let me offer some details. Inclusiveness gives every person the opportunity to learn about prevention, and then, when necessary, obtain proper diagnosis and treatment. The lack of access for millions of Americans is a national tragedy, and a preventable one. Access is the foundation for a new covenant in American healthcare. Improving access does not mean reducing standards of care. We start in a strong position. Most Americans already have access to quality healthcare, but the nation must now focus on those who do not. The payoff for greater inclusion and access will come in a healthier, more productive America.

I believe that the best system is one in which each individual is informed and empowered to choose from the widest spectrum of opportunities. Such a system is neither imposed from the top by coercive authority, nor settled by the lowest common denominator in pursuit of the lowest costs.

Individualized

America's culture honors the right of an individual to make choices. Our healthcare system should also honor that individuality. That means America's healthcare system should be based on the freedom to choose. Such a system wells up from the coordinated actions of a multitude of individuals acting in enlightened self-interest.

I believe a system in which people are able to make individual choices is resilient enough to respond to constant change. People who benefit from such a healthcare system develop an allegiance to it and use it wisely. One requirement is that such a system be universal. If a system puts the minority at a disadvantage, then that minority will not support the system.

Healthcare is not a commodity. In fact, it's the most personalized of services, and it varies because every patient is unique. If you think that all healthcare is alike, and that all doctors are the same, then it might make sense to treat healthcare as a commodity. But that's not my experience. Individualized healthcare allows doctors and patients to choose the best courses of care rather than settling for the lowest common denominator or "one-size-fits-all" medicine.

Some things will have to change. The big issue is the control of healthcare. This issue needs to be debated. Meanwhile, we can work on specific parts of the individualized agenda. For example, who owns your children's immunization records? When schools or camps need proof that kids have had their shots, why should parents have to make a written request that takes days to process? I believe people should have access to their medical records on confidential, password-protected Web sites.

Our healthcare system has numerous players: doctors, nurses, hospitals, pharmaceutical companies, insurance companies, employers, and many others. But all of them exist for one reason: to serve the individual patient with personalized services. Any system that fails to put the interests of the individual patient first is asking the individual to serve the system. Empowered consumers will not tolerate such a system.

Individualized healthcare also imposes more personal responsibility on the individual. The bottom line is that people are expected to bear the primary responsibility for managing their own health in consultation with their physicians. The Statue of Liberty in New York City harbor is one of my favorite sights in the world. Maybe we need a Statue of Responsibility in San Francisco Harbor. Such a counterbalance would emphasize the complementary nature of liberty and accountability. We can't have one without the other.[5] I will have more to say about personal responsibility and healthcare in Chapter 9.

Innovative

Innovation is the key to continued success in finding new treatments and cures. American ingenuity is the world's best hope for a better future in healthcare. Most of the world's innovations in healthcare—medicines, diagnostic systems, research breakthroughs in wellness and prevention—come stamped "Discovered in America." Americans can be justly proud of this achievement even as we are concerned about forces that will take the teeth out of America's ability to continue innovating.

Innovation-driven healthcare is clearly going to be one of the growth industries of the twenty-first century, and America has this part absolutely right. European research labs used to discover most of the world's prescription medicines. Today, Europe accounts for less than 40 percent of new medicines, and that level of discovery is declining. The United States once discovered 20-30 percent of new drugs; now it is over 60 percent. The United States has an enormous competitive advantage in the business of healthcare, in medical devices, in medical training, and in pharmaceutical R&D. This is a great resource we can pass on to our grandchildren if we don't accidentally destroy it.

Information-Driven

Information is the most underestimated component of the healthcare system and the component with the most potential to align the system with prevention, early diagnosis, and early intervention.

The Internet revolution is bringing down the curtain on those who believe that denying patients access to information is a way to control costs. That approach was never right and has become impossible in this new, wired world. To help conquer the cost of disease, a new American healthcare system must give people access to clear and timely information.

The principal product of the pharmaceutical industry is information. Ours is the ultimate knowledge industry. If I put a white tablet in your hand, it would be absolutely useless to you unless you understood what it was for, its indications and contraindications, dosage, and drug interactions. It's a very long list. Discovery and development of a new drug is more about generating this information than identifying a new molecular entity. That white tablet is devoid of value unless it is bundled with the information that we spend billions of dollars generating.

Receiving the best healthcare hinges on the willingness of every participant in the system to be accountable to the patient. To make this commitment meaningful requires that trained professionals have the most up-to-date information about you and your medical history. It also requires that you have the most up-to-date information about your providers, their services, fee schedule, and clinical outcomes.

The system must give larger platforms to those who advocate for patients—the vanguard of helping improve the nation's approaches to both medical care and humanity in healthcare. The system must also help free medical professionals from excessive bureaucracy and help them avoid mistakes in serving patients. An information-driven system will create informed patients, educated advocates, and focused healthcare professionals. I say more about healthcare information technology in Chapter 11.

Incentivized

The cost of prevention and wellness is small in relation to the suffering, misery, and economic toll of chronic disease and trauma. Through a new focus on prevention, wellness, early diagnosis, and treatment, Americans will earn the largest payoff for the dollars they invest in healthcare.

The incentives I am talking about are those that shift the healthcare system from an emphasis on cost management to a focus on wellness, prevention, swift diagnosis, and early treatment. It will not be an easy transition. As it has currently evolved, the medical system is neither financially rewarded nor intellectually disciplined for a shift to this wellness-focused model of health and healthcare. Rather, it is addicted to a model of acute care that swings into action when sick patients present their symptoms.

The medical system will respond to signals that it's no longer business as usual. Our job as a society is to present incentives that reward practitioners who add to the wellness of patients. For example, rewards must come into play to let physicians understand that activities in support of nutrition, diet, and exercise are just as important as providing acute interventions and procedures.

I believe in fixing the problem, not fixing blame. The current healthcare system is staffed by talented people with the best of intentions. It's the way we finance the system, the way we pay for procedures, and the imbalance in tax incentives within the healthcare system that need to be addressed. In other words, we need to replace the old incentives with a new set that is more tightly aligned with the outcomes we desire.

This new set of incentives also applies to patients. Patients must be encouraged to be self-aware, educated, and responsible for behaviors that impact their health and the health of others. Patients will have the tools to self-manage any chronic conditions they might have. I prefer incentives that reward positive behavior rather than punishments for negative behavior, but a full measure of personal responsibility means that educated, self-aware consumers of healthcare must accept the consequences of their choices.

Looking Ahead

Changing America's focus to a healthcare system that is inclusive, individualized, innovative, information-driven, and includes incentives inclined toward wellness and prevention is only the first step toward returning patients to the center of care. When moving forward, reformers must place a maximum value on good health, and focus on lowering the cost of disease. Healthcare should empower individuals to take responsibility for their own healthcare decisions, on the assumption that individuals spending their own money are in the best position to make wise choices.

The new system should also help Americans save for their own healthcare and should offer comparable tax benefits to those without access to employer-based health insurance. Further, it should expand the safety net programs to meet the needs of Americans who cannot afford coverage.

The traditional course that threatens to bankrupt us is focused on imposing arbitrary cost constraints. The emerging healthcare system should focus instead on maintaining wellness and improving overall patient outcomes. It should build on the latest advances in both bio-medical and information technology, while stressing individualized care for individual conditions. It should promote continued research and development in medical innovation, including ways to reduce depression, violence, and suicide. In short, the system should be evaluated on the basis of the value it creates.

America's healthcare must also promote efficiencies in the delivery of healthcare. Currently, the cost of administration, unneeded treatment, and outright fraud siphons off 30 percent of our healthcare investments. That's three times more than we spend on medicines. The best way to get these expenditures in harmony and to promote process efficiencies and eliminate waste in the healthcare value chain is through the discipline of competition. As I suggested in Chapter 7, competition has proved to be the most powerful force in the world for increasing quality and decreasing costs.

Reforms in healthcare must be supported by reforms in other basic infrastructures that contribute to and guarantee our well-being. Included in this is the unreasonable cost of medical liability coverage. Today, help for those with genuine grievances is overdue because our medical malpractice system is out of control. As a result, defensive medicine has become necessary—driving up costs and driving both doctors and innovators out of healthcare. The days of jackpot justice must end. Reform must include a system that speeds justice and compensation to those who have been injured, while accounting for the reasonable risks that must be taken in the course of any treatment.

Florida: A Healthy State

One of every 10 Americans suffers from chronic disease. Medical costs for people with chronic diseases account for more than 70 percent of the $1 trillion spent on healthcare each year in the United States. As in many parts of the country, low-income Floridians with chronic illnesses seek care designed to treat acute symptoms rather than addressing the underlying causes.

In order to be a Medicaid beneficiary, you must be poor and sick. This is a devastating combination. In the haste to locate a provider for their symptoms, Medicaid patients often end up using the emergency room for primary-care services, an expensive, inefficient solution that drives up the overall cost of healthcare. In fact, Medicaid patients are more than twice as likely as other non-Medicaid patients with the same type of illnesses to be admitted to the hospital via the emergency room because of an acute event.

I'm not content with recommending a course of action unless I have personal experience that it works. In this book and in my speeches, I have insisted that a coordinated emphasis on wellness, education, prevention, and early intervention is superior to cost avoidance and rationing as the best way to put health and fiscal discipline back into the world's healthcare systems. But how do I know my strategy promotes health while saving money? I looked for an opportunity to be a partner in a pilot program to find out one way or another.

A popular definition of insanity is doing the same thing over and over and expecting different results. The behavior of the healthcare industry meets this definition. Virtually every state is struggling with the cost of their Medicaid programs, yet Medicaid administrators continue to pursue failed cost-control and rationing strategies.

Pfizer is in the middle of a new prevention- and education-based disease-management pilot program called *Florida: A Healthy State.*

The State of Florida, operating the fourth largest Medicaid program in the United States, faced a $650 million Medicaid budget shortfall in 2001. Florida's Medicaid spending has nearly doubled in just six years. More than 22 cents of every state dollar is consumed by healthcare. In response, Florida, like virtually every state, saves money by negotiating price concessions from its healthcare providers. From the pharmaceutical companies, Florida has extracted especially tough price concessions.

In designing *Florida: A Healthy State*, we sought to demonstrate that taxpayers and healthcare recipients in Florida could get more healthcare value through a prevention-based, disease management paradigm, rather than through price controls. We suggested a coordinated program designed to shift the State's focus from the costs of medicines and healthcare to the costs of disease. Florida Governor Jeb Bush understood right away that this was more than about changing words. It represented a new paradigm for looking at the problem.

We proposed a program that would move chronically ill Medicaid patients away from emergency rooms and give them a better option to leverage the benefits of education, prevention in the form of behavior modification, and early intervention. For example, diabetes, one of the most destructive diseases we know, responds well to even modest behavioral lifestyle changes. The program would partner patients with trained medical professionals who could offer the kind of individualized and personal care that they never had before. The program would include patient education, innovative nursing care, and counseling on diet, exercise, and smoking cessation, as well as other lifestyle changes. My point was that if we could get these high-risk patients out of emergency rooms, where they were often seen as hindrances, and into the hands of caregivers, we could do more to help them at less cost to the state.

Florida: A Healthy State emerged as a unique public-private partnership between Florida's Agency for Health Care Administration and Pfizer. The statewide program's main objective is to reduce the terrible burden of illness on the state's Medicaid patients, people largely disenfranchised and disempowered by the current system.

Florida: A Healthy State was launched in 2001. It was a thrill to be in the room when Governor Jeb Bush looked at his director of Medicaid and said, "No, we're not going to do business as usual. There's got to be a better way." The governor had to fight for an idea that improves health outcomes and saves money. The state's Medicaid professionals and many legislators were opposed to a prevention-based approach because they believe they can get more cost reductions with price controls. Well, they're wrong, they can't, and I was willing to bet that if given a chance, a program like *Florida: A Healthy State* would prove it.

In operation, a network of 55 care managers at 10 local hospitals taps into the experience and resources of community organizations and local physicians across the state. These specially trained and supported care managers reach more than 150,000 high-risk patients on a consistent basis to help them better navigate the healthcare system, connect and interact with physicians, understand their health conditions, and take positive steps to stay healthy. The program employs a patient-centered health approach for Medicaid beneficiaries suffering from heart failure, diabetes, hypertension, asthma, and any related morbidities. A secondary goal of the program is to map the intensity of the care treatment to the individual's disease and risk severity.

In nearly all cases, individuals in the program have received more medical attention for their conditions than ever before. The program also touches an additional 76,000 lower-risk patients through a broad array of educational interventions and 24-hour telephonic nursing support. The program has delivered more than 16,000 home health aids such as blood pressure cuffs for hypertensive patients, weight scales for heart failure patients, and peak flow meters and spacers for asthmatics, while coordinating care with providers, conducting home visits, and monitoring clinical measures.

The State of Florida announced that the program reached nearly 150,000 Medicaid beneficiaries and improved their health while saving the state $42 million. That's 27 percent more first-year savings than Pfizer promised when it started the program in 2001. For the sickest 20,000 people, trips to emergency rooms dropped 5.7 percent, and hospital stays fell 9.7 percent. This drop in emergency room utilization represents real savings to the state. Readers who are interested in specific clinical and financial outcomes of the program can find details at www.pfizer.com. This is the kind of public-private partnership that I believe holds the key to progress.

We are now partnering with Humana to demonstrate a better way of managing 15,000 elderly patients with diabetes and congestive heart failure. We hope to show that this kind of public-private partnership can improve the health and well-being of patients with chronic diseases while reducing the overall cost of care. What both of these partnerships have in common is a focus on health improvement rather than cost management.

Weighing the Difference

I am proud that we have impacted the lives of so many Floridians. Their letters are full of gratitude and hope. They describe how refreshing it was to receive attention that was personal and individualized from professionals who cared about their staying healthy instead of just treating them when they were sick. One story told to me really stands out as a validation of why the program has been so successful. It involves a diabetic resident of Florida—let's call her Ruby—and the counselor she met at the hospital during one of her many visits. I share the story as a model of what it means to keep the patient at the center of the equation.

The counselor suggested that Ruby enroll in the *Florida: A Healthy State* approach and, with her physician's enthusiastic blessing, she joined the program. Together Ruby and the counselor began to lay out a road map to manage her lifelong condition, which like many diabetics, included a struggle with obesity.

The counselor indicated to Ruby that even a 10-percent reduction in body weight would bring huge benefits in her health. "Do you think we can do that?" the counselor asked. Ruby nodded doubtfully.

The counselor continued. "Ruby, it's not that hard if we set a goal of losing just two pounds a week. You can weigh yourself every week and we will see real progress." Ruby continued to look doubtful. It took some time, but the counselor finally understood that Ruby was not really arguing about the need to lose weight. There was something else. It turned out that Ruby didn't own a bathroom scale and didn't want to admit she couldn't afford one.

In that poignant moment, I got a glimpse of all the obstacles that this woman had been battling. The counselor was determined not to abandon this woman. With the patient's words still hanging in the air, the counselor took $20 out of program funds, drove to a drugstore, and bought Ruby the first bathroom scale she had ever owned. The last time I heard from the counselor, Ruby was fine and on track in reducing her weight.

No gatekeepers, no arguing over whether or not bathroom scales were covered under the health plan. There was just a caring counselor, willing to listen, and moving toward creating health in a patient-centered, wellness-oriented manner. This is better healthcare at lower cost. It's also plain common sense.

The *Florida: A Healthy State* initiative has met all the goals set for its first three years, and it has been renewed through 2005. We believe this approach could be an important model in reforming the healthcare system throughout the United States, and elsewhere.

Pushback

I expected pushback from the state's healthcare establishment, and I wasn't disappointed. Although the original two-year agreement was extended until September 2005, the Florida Legislature demonstrated its willingness to embrace failed price-control strategies. Lawmakers banned the linking of care-management programs such as *Florida: A Healthy State* to preferential treatment on the state's Medicaid preferred-drug list. In other words, the legislators wanted not only the guarantees of health management, but the deep discounts of price controls, as well.

We demonstrated in Florida that if you work with chronically ill patients to manage all aspects of their illnesses, and make the best medicines available as part of that effort, the result will be healthier, more productive people at lower cost to the state. It is not an easy conclusion for the state to accept. The answer is not in rationing or wage and price controls, but in prevention and wellness.

If we're really worried about the high cost of disease, we must become concerned about changing patient behaviors. With the baby boom generation now in their 50s and 60s, we just can't afford to treat people at the level that will be required without fundamental changes in the system, focusing on prevention and wellness.

Other useful healthcare models are emerging as well, and I welcome anything that promises benefits. What is important is that we shift focus from the cost of care to the cost of disease, so that emerging models have a chance to work.

We currently have a healthcare system that treats the patient as the recipient of an entitlement, does not reward restraint, and disempowers the individual. We know that such a system is doomed to a cycle of rising costs and lowered expectations. Yet we hesitate to replace this system with an approach we suspect will work better when we invoke the mantra "health is different." After all, shouldn't everyone, rich or poor, have access to healthcare?

Indeed, that is my position. Throughout this book, I have advocated nothing less than a healthcare system that includes everyone, regardless of the ability to pay. The fallacy is concluding that if health is fundamental and must be available to all, than health must be provided by employers or the government alone. Maybe there are ways other than centralized, government-provided programs to meet the basic needs of people, including their health.

CONSUMER-DRIVEN HEALTHCARE: BALANCING CHOICE, RESPONSIBILITY, AND ACCOUNTABILITY

M ost present-day attempts at healthcare reform can lead only to mediocrity. Whatever the intended destination, the road signs are all marked "price controls," "rationing," and "government regulation." These roads lead to dead ends, and I believe there is a better way.

I start with the patient at the center. A system that prizes life as the supreme value acknowledges that, by definition, the central figure whose interests are paramount must be the individual seeking care. Thus a patient is the ultimate decision maker, most knowledgeable about his or her individual health choices, and the ultimate arbiter of value. A society's healthcare system must be individualized. Such a system allows doctors and patients to choose the best courses of care rather than settling for the lowest common denominator of "average care for the average person." The design and the outcomes of every element of the healthcare system should be measured against the well-being of the patient.

On the other hand, unless the patient and the doctor make decisions at least partially based on cost, either prices will spiral out of control or services will be rationed. In a properly functioning healthcare system, patients would be able to consider costs and trade-offs in selecting procedures and services. Individuals make personal decisions about the shoes they wear, the restaurants they frequent, and the cars they drive.

They have actionable information about prices and quality on which to make these decisions. Price is not always the determining factor, but it is always considered.

I envision nothing less robust for consumers of healthcare. An efficient healthcare system would be characterized by transparency in public and private sectors alike. Neither the details of restrictions in services nor costs must be hidden from consumers. They might wish to trade cost for a more limited menu of physicians or pay more for greater access to specialists or choice of medicines. This would be their decision. There is ample evidence that patients, given adequate information, can make rational choices about their own healthcare.

I further believe that the only way to fix healthcare is to eliminate the three-way system that exists today, with a patient consuming services, a healthcare professional providing treatment, and a third party paying the bills. The new model must feature a two-way system grounded by the patient and his or her healthcare professionals. Intermediaries sustain the illusion that someone else is paying for our healthcare, that in some important sense, the costs are borne by someone else. As humorist P. J. O'Rourke observes, "If you think healthcare is expensive now, wait until it's free."

Throughout this book I have suggested that the cornerstone of healthcare reform is to empower consumers of health services with as much information and market power as possible. The best way I know to create empowered patients is through the creation of incentivized personal health accounts that unleash the benefits of an ownership society. When I walked the streets of Budapest, Hungary in 1979 during the last days of Soviet domination, it was still possible to see the bullet holes from World War II on building walls. As long as the state owned the buildings, tenants had no incentive to make repairs. Less than two years later, with the buildings now in private hands, property owners quickly filled in the holes and painted. Only when each of us owns the healthcare resources we control, can we hope to build in the responsibility, restraint, and market dynamics that will end the combination of rising costs and declining quality.

Personal health accounts certainly did not originate with me. They are an outgrowth of two major economic shifts that are changing the social contract between employers and employees. The first trend is the transition from defined benefit to defined contribution retirement plans. The emergence of 401(k) retirement plans is part of this shift. The second trend is the transition from employer-provided healthcare to individually purchased plans. Health Savings Accounts (HSAs) were enabled by Congress in the Medicare Prescription Drug Improvement and Modernization Act of 2003, and President George W. Bush includes them in his healthcare reform proposal. Many varieties of these accounts have been proposed, and they are known by a number of names.

What's important is the ability for consumers to take ownership of their healthcare destinies. Health Savings Accounts (HSAs) allow consumers, within limits, to choose how their healthcare money is invested; they give us incentives for shopping around for the best value, and brings market forces into play so we are paying actual costs for the healthcare services we use. If managed care provides incentives to influence physician behavior, HSAs provide incentives to influence consumer behavior.

Under most plans under discussion, you could make deposits to tax-free HSAs to finance routine healthcare expenses. If you are currently covered by employer-provided insurance, you could fund your HSA by switching from low-deductible policies to high-deductible catastrophic policies and depositing the premium savings. Furthermore, the plan would eliminate the arbitrary discrimination of today's tax system and allow all Americans, regardless of employment status, to claim tax benefits for purchasing catastrophic insurance and making deposits to HSAs. Under this empowerment model, individuals and families would be encouraged or even required to make tax-exempt deposits into health accounts.

Two salutary benefits of this system result. First, the pool of savings created under this approach would be invested to the ultimate benefit of the economy as a whole, not just the healthcare sector. This is because investment in health not only fuels innovation (as in other sectors), but it also enhances productivity, and ultimately, reduces costs to consumers. It also creates jobs and adds value to the economy. Second, it provides the restraint that the present three-party system lacks.

There are many decisions to make and details to work out before HSAs can start working. This book is not the place to debate jurisdiction, financing, taxes, medical information privacy, and other thorny public policy issues that will have to be decided. But it is a platform for me to make the case for four attributes that I believe HSAs should deliver. At a minimum, HSAs should:

1. Put control over spending in the hands of individual patients
2. Allow individuals to buy benefits that are at least as comprehensive as they have today
3. Require individuals to buy a minimum catastrophic medical insurance policy for themselves and their dependents
4. Allow the individual to pocket any savings resulting from restraint and prudent behavior

The following scenarios paint a more concrete picture of HSAs in action.

Control

When you go to a doctor or get a test, you will know exactly what the service costs. If you accept the price, you will pay the doctor on the spot using your health account debit card. Because it's your money, doctors will tell you up-front what their fee is for each service. Doctors will understand that if some other doctor provides the same service for a lower fee, or better service for the same fee, they will face an empty waiting room. Bringing market forces to play will push costs down as healthcare providers compete for patient dollars.

An added benefit is that real money is freed up when you pay for services when rendered. Doctors will no longer have to hire clerical people to fill out all the forms, chase after your insurance provider, compute your copay, and send out the bills. The doctor can apply those savings to lowering costs or improving customer services. Some estimate savings from this step alone as high as 30 percent.[1]

HSA plans give you a direct financial incentive to spend prudently on healthcare because you are spending your own money. Furthermore, the plan extends the same tax advantages to all Americans, unlike the current system, which discriminates against the unemployed, the self-employed, and employees of small businesses that do not offer health insurance. Ensuring tax fairness goes a long way toward making health-care affordable for people who are now without health insurance.

Comprehensive

In making the transition to an HSA-oriented world, you should not be penalized in any way. Your healthcare will be at least as robust as it is today, preferably better. And because you do not have to pay for a plan or for extra coverage that you do not want, plans will become more customized as providers compete on the basis of particular services and price.

The healthcare system will unleash new levels of innovation to compete for the millions of Americans ready to spend their HSA dollars. Bureaucracies will adapt existing healthcare models such as managed care or fee-for-service plans to compete for these dollars. Why should the fee-for-service physician practice be the dominant form of providing ambulatory care? New service variations on HMOs or preferred provider organizations will be offered to and chosen—or rejected—by the individual. Brand new approaches will evolve. For example, some doctors might offer concierge services, under which you would prepay an annual fee and in exchange get healthcare for no additional cost. And, yes, the fee-for-service practice will continue. The only difference is that you will know in advance what the fee is and will make your decision with all the relevant facts at your fingertips.

A thousand choices would flourish. You would buy services that, in your view, not in the view of some politician or healthcare administrator, would serve you and your family best. You would find existing procedures offered individually or bundled with value-added services. Preventive, prepaid, boutique healthcare services will materialize. Whichever level of quality you deemed most suitable, you would find it available at the least possible cost. This would be so because individuals would have the most incentive to preserve the value of their HSA balances. Without copays or insurance intermediaries, people would have no more illusion that the money came from anywhere but their own pockets.

Catastrophic Medical Insurance

The first purchase you make out of your HSA is a high-deductible catastrophic medical insurance policy. Purchasing such a plan would be mandatory. Such plans help to reduce the premium but still provide protection from unexpected, catastrophic healthcare expenses. You will pay for most routine healthcare directly out of your HSA. This insurance policy will kick into action if you should have a catastrophic medical condition and you have spent down your account. Then the policy will pay for 100 percent of your medical expenses.

Healthcare reform proposals that focus on catastrophic care could go a long way toward relieving emergency rooms and other healthcare providers of an enormous financial burden, as well as closing the health outcome gap. Catastrophic insurance premiums with a high deductible are relatively inexpensive when compared with more comprehensive plans. I recognize that not everyone will be able to afford even the relatively modest premiums of such policies. A program to subsidize catastrophic insurance could give real substance to the political goal of restraining spiraling healthcare expenses. When people experience major health emergencies, such insurance offers peace of mind that lifesaving treatments will be provided and that families will not be thrown into financial disarray.

Why should you be forced to buy a minimum level of catastrophic health insurance? On one level, it is a protection for society. The community should be able to limit individual choice so as to ensure that no individual, due to irresponsibility or accident, is without insurance and thus becomes a burden to society.

This conclusion flows from my understanding of personal responsibility as the flip side of liberty. If the HSA-approach represents individual liberty, the mandate to buy a minimum catastrophic medical insurance policy represents responsibility. I think of the situation as I do about automobile insurance. Most of us know it's safer to slow down and drive defensively. Yet we are at liberty to drive our cars faster than posted speed limits. We also accept that if we get too many speeding tickets or by our negligence hurt others, we'll pay more for our car insurance and eventually we might lose the privilege of driving altogether. If we want to drive, a certain minimum level of liability insurance is required to protect those whom our choices might impact. Note that car insurance is government mandated but privately delivered, the same model I advocate for delivering healthcare insurance.

Automobile insurance companies obviously wish to insure only safe, law-abiding drivers. If they deem our driving habits unacceptably risky, they will raise our premiums. Ultimately, they will not issue a policy to us at any affordable price. If so, we would be prevented from legally driving an automobile on public roads. This seems fair for a privilege such as driving, especially if the converse holds, as well. Safe, law-abiding drivers should get discounts on premiums.

Health insurance is different from car insurance in fundamental ways. We don't want individuals to be denied health insurance because insurance companies want to cover only healthy people. It's unfair to raise premiums or deny health insurance to people when they get sick. Such medical underwriting practice is called "cherry picking" and is a process—I'm only slightly joking—by which anyone who has ever visited a doctor is excluded from coverage.

Nevertheless, I see merit in the idea of making health insurance mandatory, like car insurance. Such a step would have two implications. First, it would capture the "healthy uninsured," whose absence from the insurance pool makes insurance costlier for all the people who seek insurance because they presumably have something wrong with them. This plan would work only if accompanied by a subsidy for people who couldn't afford it and letting the federal government act as a reinsurer. I will say more about the uninsurability problem in Chapter 13.

But it's the second implication I would like to discuss here. Perhaps there is something about the intersection of personal responsibility and health insurance that we can take from the car insurance experience. By requiring people to obtain affordable health insurance, we create new opportunities for people to promote their health and control health costs through prevention-oriented personal choices.

Most of us know that our health depends to a large degree on personal behaviors around diet, exercise, and nutrition. Yet we are at liberty to live a medically high risk life and practice whatever level of eating, smoking, and inactivity we desire. We must also understand that in so choosing, we will spend more of our disposable income on our insurance premiums. Insurance companies should have the right to base insurance premiums partly on personal behaviors. If you have hypertension and reject the prudent measures—diet, exercise, and drug treatment—recommended by your physician to control it, at least some of the financial consequences of that decision should be yours.

Personal responsibility is not totally controlling. Genetics and random chance also play critical roles in determining health. My hope is not that we "punish the victim" but that we create meaningful links between personal health habits and outcomes.

Let's say you work for Pfizer. As I noted in Chapter 3, Pfizer pays approximately $7850 a year to provide an employee and his or her family with health insurance coverage. Under this approach, we would deposit this amount into your HSA for you to invest and use to pay for your ordinary healthcare expenses. This account would join your other savings and retirement accounts that you manage. You would be encouraged to make additional contributions to these accounts. Pfizer would no longer be an intermediary between you and your healthcare professional.

Overall healthcare costs might or might not absolutely decrease, because aging populations and technological advances tend to push costs up, notes Wilfried Prewo, an analyst for the Centre for the New Europe. "But whatever the total costs we will have, they will be at the minimum for the level of care desired by society and markedly below the cost trend of the current system," he says.[2]

I happen to believe that healthcare spending will rise. That alarms some policymakers, but why should it? Spending on information and communications technology has similarly soared over the past decade, yet no one speaks of a "computer crisis" or a "mobile phone crisis."

The increased spending for these technologies is not a crisis because people recognize the value of these technologies. Another factor is that individuals—not governments or third parties—pay for their computers and mobile phones. Technology vendors understand that consumers expect real value for their investments, that price is often the key consideration, and that consumers will quickly switch vendors for a better deal. The result? Costs have gone down steadily, quality has improved, and access to the technologies has increased. Despite the highly technical character of these products, consumers routinely navigate the system and make informed choices.

And all this has transpired without the intervention of a one-size-fits-all government-provided technology insurance program. There is every reason to believe that similar results would be seen in healthcare if a real market were allowed to operate.

Accumulate Savings

This is explicitly not "use it or lose it." Whatever money remains in your HSA at the end of the year remains there and continues to build up tax-free interest over time—you get to keep what you do not spend. Portability means the HSA follows you from employer to employer. You would be able to accumulate substantial savings over your working career, which you could use upon retirement or leave to your children as part of your estate.

The vast majority of Americans would greatly benefit from the combination of less-expensive, high-deductible policies and HSAs. In any given year, most Americans have no, or modest, medical expenses, and 94 percent have medical expenses under $3000. Under such a system, your maximum personal exposure every year is capped by your catastrophic policy; meanwhile, your savings to meet that possible exposure keep accumulating every year with interest. In other words, the deck is stacked in favor of your coming out ahead.

HSAs would be of particular help to employees and their families when money was tight. Even today's low deductibles, particularly when combined with copayments, can create hardship for those struggling to make ends meet. With HSAs, money would be available to pay the first dollar of medical costs—no deductibles, no copayments. In addition, people who were between jobs could use their HSAs to buy insurance coverage. About half the people who are uninsured remain that way for four months or less; typically, they are between jobs that they rely on to provide their families with health insurance benefits. The accumulated savings in HSAs would be available to tide people over during such times.

For employees, the advantages of this approach are enormous: they actually get more money in cash (tax-free, interest-bearing cash) than they lose in employer-provided insurance coverage—even during the first year. Over time, unused savings continue to build up with tax-free compound interest.

Many people are skeptical about the HSA-empowerment model. Let me anticipate some objections.

The average consumer lacks the medical knowledge to make sound judgments about their healthcare.

That's why we hire experts. Most people make sound judgments about purchasing, driving, and maintaining their automobiles without being required to know what's under the hood. We learn through experience and word-of-mouth which car dealers and garages provide real value, and which ones don't. Sometimes we make the wrong choice and are disappointed. We take our business elsewhere and tell our friends. We become smarter through experience. We learn that it is less expensive to maintain a car (prevention) than to get it repaired (go to the mechanic). Newspapers have automobile columns and advertising that educates readers about car prices and services. I anticipate a blossoming of medical columns, reviews of products and services, and other information sources, both free and by subscription, by print, broadcast, and especially Web channels.[3]

Consumers need education about not just health literacy but health benefit literacy. I know students in college who can explain the warning signs for cancer, name the four types of leukemia, and can tell you the difference between Type I and Type II diabetes. But ask them to distinguish between a copayment and a deductible and they are lost. Understanding health information is the strongest predictor of a person's health status. Children need to learn about health benefit literacy in the K-12 curriculum, perhaps as part of the physical education program.

In view of the epidemic of obesity and with higher rates of diabetes occurring in American children, I am concerned by how many governors are granting schools waivers from offering physical education. This is entirely the wrong signal. There is no better way than daily PE to support the benefits of childhood fitness as well as ongoing health and health literacy. Teaching sports skills and teamwork are important, but PE is most valuable when it develops lifetime activity habits that are consistent with good health.

People are reluctant to spend their own money so they will put off necessary healthcare, making themselves even sicker.

The idea behind this objection is that people are tightwads and will "save themselves sick." We shouldn't dismiss this objection lightly. We all know people whose cars are falling apart because they are too frugal to spend money on preventive maintenance. Would people striving to save money or preserve their HSA balances for "a rainy day" be tempted to cut down on necessary medical care and thereby make themselves or their children even sicker?

Early studies by the RAND Corporation suggested that some employees experience a reduction in health status when they become responsible for the first dollar of healthcare. But subsequent studies revealed that when given the chance, employees actually increase the utilization of preventive services. When Aetna launched a consumer-directed healthcare plan option, employees enrolled in the HSA had 23 percent more general preventive exams (mammography, colonoscopy) than under traditional plans. Gynecological exams went up 4.2 percent. Inpatient admissions went down, emergency room visits went down.[4]

People can be penny-wise and pound-foolish. Prevention education must be part of any healthcare benefit program. Ultimately, however, natural consequence is the best instructor. We don't have a government agency requiring us to change the oil in our cars every 3000 miles, yet most car owners figure out it is in their interest to do so. Ownership is the key. No one in the history of the world has ever changed the oil in a rented car. But when we think of our cars as assets, we have the ownership interest to make investments in prevention.

The same will hold true in healthcare. Through ownership of their personal health accounts, consumers will learn that deferring treatments or cutting pills in half is more costly in the long run than taking care of their health before they are sick. But if natural consequences are insufficient, the market will respond with a variety of incentives.

Incentives will take the form of carrots and sticks. The carrots will be in the form of discounts rewarding people for healthy behaviors and behaviors that advance prevention. The sticks will be price increases for risky behaviors. I believe that most people respond better to rewards than to punishment.

Healthcare providers are already offering the incentives for people to take care of themselves. Already, insurance providers such as Oak Brook, Illinois-based Destiny Health give insured members tangible rewards for living healthy lifestyles. Members who quit smoking, start an exercise program, get a flu shot, or take a CPR course earn airline miles, vacations, health-club discounts, and other rewards. Initial results: 85 percent of its members have started an exercise program within the last year, compared with 24 percent in other plans. Members are five times more likely to achieve progress toward their conditioning goals. In this, the plan helps reduce overall health-care costs.

London-based Prudential Health Limited believes that money talks. PruHealth is using cash discounts to motivate policyholders to embrace healthy behaviors and decrease risky behaviors. PruHealth has devised its Vitality program to reward members with discounted premiums if they keep themselves fit and healthy and reduce their claims. Members earn points for a range of activities such as going to the fitness center, stopping smoking, having regular health checks, or even reading health articles on PruHealth's Web site. The company is betting that it will cost them less to cover health-oriented members than people enrolled in traditional health plans, and is willing to return some of those savings to keep members fit and well. For members who really go after the benefits and do not file a claim, customers can earn a 100-percent discount on the premiums they pay.[5]

Young people think they are indestructible. They will tend to underinsure themselves and then regret it.

They might, but what exactly is the problem? On the average, young people who are healthy and take care of themselves might not need more than a minimum plan for many years. It might, in fact, be rational for young people to underinsure themselves if they apply the money they save to constructive uses.

Is it possible that, as they get older, they might regret their decision because switching later in life to a more robust plan will be more expensive? Possibly, but again, where's the problem? Those that decided on a minimum health plan in their early years have had the use—sometimes for decades—of funds that would otherwise have gone to healthcare premiums. Perhaps they have used that money to invest in education, buy a house, build up a stock portfolio, or invest in life insurance. Or perhaps they simply put it in the bank. All these assets are now available to step up to a higher-priced health plan or to pay for health services. And if they made less prudent choices with the money that left them financially exposed, the consequences of their choices are truly their own. The minimum mandatory coverage that everyone is mandated to have is the safety net that prevents a drop to welfare levels.

People are too shortsighted to be wise shoppers of health services that provide for their healthcare 30, 40, and 50 years down the road.

I believe that most people have the intelligence and imagination to make sound choices if they are empowered through education and choice. In any case, we entrust people to make many more far-reaching decisions. The decision to have children has significant long-term consequences, financial and otherwise, yet the human race has survived without this activity requiring a government license.

People can be trusted to act rationally when the money they are dealing with comes out of their own pockets. Restraint would be the order of the day as each patient weighed the cost-benefit of every procedure. A patient would be reluctant to embark on an odyssey of redundant visits to specialists because the costs of duplicate office fees and diagnostic tests would come out of his or her own account. Of course, there are no guarantees that every decision will be correct or even prudent. But at least the costs of imprudent personal behavior will not be shifted to the community at large.

This objection carries with it a strain of fear and elitism. We know this to be so because people who are skeptical about the ability of others to make healthcare decisions for the long term invariably believe that they themselves are quite capable of doing just that. The guardians of the status quo lose their elite status when the lost souls they are supposedly guiding find their own path.

You can't fool me. Consumer-directed healthcare is just a way for employers to shift proportionately more benefit liability and cost to employees.

That's exactly what employers are trying to do, but notice that in so doing, employers are shifting nothing more than what has always belonged to employees. We should also acknowledge that in shifting costs to employees, employers also shift autonomy, control, and power. These are items of inestimable value. The questions are: Do employees want that autonomy and control, and will they use the power in the service of their health and prosperity? I believe employees will accept the bargain of ownership over their health and retirement portfolios and use it wisely.

The Primacy of the Patient-Physician Relationship

Over the years, the relationship between patient and physician has evolved from something formal into something more akin to a partnership. As patients become more knowledgeable about health and health issues, doctors are welcoming their input, in turn creating a bond of trust.

As recently as 25 years ago, the relationship between patient and physician followed a paternalistic model—the doctor told the patient what to do and the patient did it. Today those paternalistic relationships have been largely replaced by relationships that are merely transactional and, increasingly, even adversarial. This is the consequence of a number of factors, most principally managed care, cost-shifting, and a medical malpractice onslaught that endangers any possibility of decent relationships between patients and their physicians. We cannot strive for a healthy society when the patient-physician relationship lacks trust.

When people of my parents' generation visited a doctor, medicine was often more art than science. Then doctors worked diligently to refine their bedside manner, as cures were often impossible and treatment had limited effect. They understood that a physician can do as much harm to a patient with the slip of a word as with the slip of a knife. More recently the interpersonal aspects of healthcare have been overshadowed by the emergence of science- and technology-driven medicine. Modern pharmaceuticals came of age during this period. No one can doubt the effectiveness of technological medicine, but the patient-physician relationship did suffer.

That's unfortunate because within these destabilizing forces, patients and physicians worldwide are redefining their relationship with each other and cohabiting a shared space of enormous power and influence. Over the past two decades, we have seen a movement away from paternalism to a mutual participation model. The relationship envisions the patient and physician sharing responsibility for making decisions and planning the course of treatment. It's hard to see how treatment for chronic illnesses such as rheumatoid arthritis can succeed with any other model as patients are solely responsible for implementing their treatment and determining its efficacy.

The centrality of the patient-physician relationship cannot be overstated. Only the family relationship eclipses it in tradition, meaning, and significance. Our research tells us that most people value the patient-physician relationship more than coworker relations, financial advisors, and, tellingly, even spiritual relations. Since the days of Hippocrates, a person's well-being was literally a private matter between the patient and the physician.[6] The element of privacy is crucial. In what other professional relationship do we literally disrobe and reveal our most vulnerable selves? So powerful is this relationship that in most countries the duty of confidentiality that physicians owe patients is enshrined in law.

What do patients really want in a medical encounter with a physician? I think the answer is as simple as it is elusive. Patients want to be able to trust their caregiver to help manage their anxiety in the face of illness. Of course, they also want competence and efficacy. They want to be able to negotiate the healthcare system effectively and to be treated with dignity and respect. Patients want to understand how their sickness or treatment will affect their lives and to learn how to care for themselves away from the clinical setting. They want to discuss the effect their illness will have on their family, friends, and finances.

To patients, doctors are not only the primary source of health information, but also the most trusted source, and the source most likely to lead to change in their behavior. Beyond delivering simple diagnosis and treatment, it is through this relationship that patients process their daily fears and worries about their health. It is the fulcrum around which healthy societies reinforce family and community linkages. These linkages provide citizens a stake in making long-term investments of human and financial resources in the community.

My own experience has convinced me that a solid alliance between patients and physicians is indispensable if we are to move our healthcare systems from an emphasis on cost control, rationing, and intervention to one of education along an increasingly prevention-oriented wellness continuum extending from birth to death. As we took a closer look at the patient-physician relationship, we realized that it was contributing three important but invisible benefits to society above and beyond diagnosis and treatment of health conditions.

The first contribution is the processing of fear and worry. Patients have concerns, and whether their worries are clinically valid or not, they have a chance to share those with the doctor. The doctor has the chance to examine the patients, do tests, counsel them on appropriate therapies, and alleviate their anxieties. That allows the patients to return to work and assume socially useful activities. It allows them to remain emotionally healthy and supports them to be good family members and productive citizens.

Second, as a doctor and a patient interact with each other, the discussions and plans and hopes that are shared reinforce very important societal bonds—those between individuals and between families and communities. A good healthcare plan takes into account the unique culture and history and relationships of the individual patient. In developing a good care plan, the doctor has to link the individuals back to their family resources and to the realities of the community in which they live.

The third requirement is that the patient-physician relationship instills a level of confidence about the future, that problems can be managed, that even if there is not a cure for the problem today, there will be a cure tomorrow. What the patient-physician relationship does is to establish a sense of long-term confidence in the future. Confidence is extremely important in terms of making financial investments, deciding whether or not it's appropriate to get married, deciding whether or not it's a reasonable thing to buy a house or bring children into the world.

Here we see the flipside of the truism that a nation without health is a nation without wealth. Obviously, workers weakened and debilitated by illness cannot achieve the productivity required to create wealth. But the lack of health has another insidious outcome. It robs a society of the confidence required to make investments in its own future.

For that reason, I suggest we think of the healthcare system as a collective. When we pay money for the healthcare system, we like to think we are investing in new pharmaceutical medicines, clinical procedures, diagnostic approaches, and hospitals. All of these are important, but the collective is bigger.

Every day throughout the world, there are literally billions of encounters in this collective as patients discharge much of their fear and worry about the health issues that confront them. In individualizing their care, doctors reinforce the importance of the connections between individuals, family, and community. By offering their humanity, physicians create an important element of community. There are not many infrastructures that can compete with this one in terms of overall scope and reach.

Though uneven in places, the infrastructure of this collective is pervasive, relatively accessible, grassroots-oriented, the people who staff it are reasonably well trained, and it is available 24 hours a day, seven days a week, throughout the world. If you take this collective away, it's reasonable to ask the question, "How much money would be required to replace it?"

I like to think that Pfizer brings some important insights about the workings of the patient-physician relationship to the table. Our most critical role is to provide the medicines that are necessary for doctors and patients to be successful. The doctors and patients must have access to these medicines in order to fight and prevent disease; otherwise they are trapped in a medical demilitarized zone with no weapons to fight disease.

We also bring an expertise in behavioral modification to the table. Educational programs that will help patients and their families and doctors as coaches and leaders of the healthcare team have been championed by Pfizer Health Solutions. Strategies and programs that we help develop can allow patients to move toward early diagnosis and adoption of healthful behaviors like exercise, good diet, and risk prevention. This investment in behavioral modification, as demonstrated in the *Florida: A Healthy State* project, not only saves money but also maintains the quality of patients' lives in the face of chronic disease.

CHAPTER 10

THE RESEARCH IMPERATIVE: THE SEARCH FOR CURES

There's a legend concerning Henry Ford that describes one approach to innovation. As the developer of the enormously popular Model T car, Ford was so focused on cost control and process that he sometimes lost sight of the customers he served. He routinely instructed his vast army of lieutenants to scour America's junkyards for discarded Model Ts to determine precisely which parts of the vehicle failed most often. If you think his goal was improving quality and that he was looking for points of failure to correct, you'd be right. But Henry Ford was looking for something else, as well.

When the junkyard detail reported back to Ford, he was not only interested in the parts that *failed*, but also in the parts that *never* failed. In fact, the Model T sported one such part. The universal joint was by far the Model T's best-designed and most reliable part. It seemed indestructible. But instead of insisting that every other part be engineered to the same standard, Ford instructed his engineers to cut back on the quality and investment in universal joint design and development. Henry Ford hated the idea that a component was better than it had to be.

Who knew that Henry Ford was a managed-care type of guy? Ford would fit easily into today's cost-driven healthcare environment in which the goal is to make every part just good enough, but no better.

This story reminds me of two things. First, process is critical to drug discovery, but it's the ultimate outcome generated by that process that justifies the painstaking struggle in which thousands of scientists screen tens of thousands of chemicals against specific disease targets. Working at the molecular level, we conduct round after round of testing, only to find that an overwhelming majority of them are unsuitable for the task in humans. I hold out the conviction that hidden in the billions of possibilities there is that one entity that will throw light on the darkness.

I also never want to forget that all this process is for the benefit of our ultimate customers, the individual patients who are depending on us. Their hopes and dreams are tied to good health, and, increasingly, their good health is tied to the ability of Pfizer and other pharmaceutical companies to research and innovate.

Will you come with me for a moment inside our research laboratories where 12,000 scientists work? Most of those researchers joined the pharmaceutical industry because they wanted to devote their lives to curing disease and alleviating suffering. Many of them have a sign in their labs that says, "Remember, the patient is waiting."

The reality that most researchers accept is that, but for a handful blessed by fate, most of them have signed on for careers of chronic futility. Only a select few will ever touch a winning drug. I can tell you that within Pfizer, the researchers who have identified a compound that actually evolved into a medicine are viewed as near-mythic figures because there are so few of them. That's the price you take on when you tackle almost impossible odds.

We can learn only from our "attrition" or failures. The reality is that our successes are too few to teach us much. When I became CEO, the failure rate of our labs was 98 percent. Only two out of every 100 molecules we invested in made it through the pipeline, and that still didn't guarantee a viable product on the other end.

I have reason to think we are getting smarter about the process of doing large-scale pharmaceutical research. In an effort to increase the survivability of Pfizer projects, 600 of our top scientists are trying to determine why so many compounds flunk in clinical trials. We call our effort to improve the process of development Attrition Task Force II (ATFII). Separate ATFII teams visited each of our worldwide labs, interviewed researchers, identified best practices, compiled their findings, and recommended changes. We are currently implementing these changes, and I believe they will increase the odds that a few more Pfizer researchers will emerge winners in the R&D lottery. The bottom line is that if we can figure out how to fail 96 percent of the time rather than 98 percent of the time, we will have doubled our productivity. Pretty sobering, isn't it?

The goals we've set for ourselves are supremely challenging. Unlocking the secrets of disease states and the molecular mechanisms needed to reverse them requires, by definition, working at the limits of human understanding and achievement.

No one relishes the brute force model that the pharmaceutical industry uses to develop medicines. No one likes spending 10 years or more and hundreds of millions of dollars on every new product, only to see the vast majority of them fail along the way. If there were a cheaper and better way to develop medicines, I promise you I'd be at the head of the line. By investment, partnering, and acquisition, we are exploring the general utility of new technologies that will perhaps take some of the serendipity out of drug discovery.

But scientific progress has always come this way: slowly, incrementally—and with success at the pinnacle inevitably built upon a rock pile of failure. When I think about the odds against us, I am reminded of what the poet Rainer Maria Rilke said: "The purpose of life is to be defeated by greater and greater things."[1] We move ahead, slowly but surely, expanding scientific knowledge with every failure, and sometimes we must be content with that victory.

Growing Threats, Shrinking Resources

For most of human history, infectious disease was a constant reminder of man's fragility. Then, starting in the years running up to World War II, the world entered a golden period in which, one by one, the infectious diseases of the world were humbled. Smallpox and scarlet fever were virtually wiped out. In the developed world, vaccines and antibiotics kept deaths from chicken pox, measles, and tuberculosis as concerns of generations past. Polio, a disease still within the memory of many adults, was wiped out in the 1950s.

Human triumph over these killers seemed so complete that in 1967, Surgeon General William H. Stewart reportedly announced it was "time to close the book on infectious diseases, declare the war against pestilence won, and shift national resources to such chronic problems as cancer and heart disease."[2]

Unfortunately, infectious disease insists on keeping the book open a little longer. By 1992, the US Institute of Medicine warned that "infectious diseases were a tangible threat to our security and that we might soon regret the comfort and complacency that had overtaken us with the advent of wonder drugs and vaccines." In 2002, instead of a change for the better, the problem of infectious diseases had gotten worse.[3]

We are threatened not only by entirely new strains of bacteria and deadly viruses, but by older strains that have mutated into antibacterial and antiretroviral resistant organisms. And then there's the incalculable threat of bioterrorism—that is, the deliberate spread of virulent and contagious organisms with the intent to harm, kill, and cause social disruption. Meanwhile, the resources the government and the pharmaceutical industry have devoted to infectious disease have been steadily decreasing over the years. According to the Institute of Medicine, all but four large pharmaceutical companies had dropped or dramatically cut back on their antibiotic research programs by 2002.[4]

Pfizer is one of a handful of pharmaceutical companies that has increased its research efforts in antimicrobials. The challenges of antibiotic research are significant because of the ability of bacteria to mutate and develop drug-resistant strains, confounding the best efforts of medical researchers. Developing antimicrobials is like trying to hit a tiny moving target while bouncing along on a galloping horse. Microbes have a way of mutating so that an antimicrobial that is effective for one person is ineffective for someone else.

The business case for developing antibiotics is not attractive. Antibiotics yield relatively little profit for manufacturers, compared to drugs that target chronic conditions such as hypertension, anemia, HIV, and hepatitis. Patients with chronic health ailments tend to take a medicine for months or years to control symptoms. Antibiotics are usually so effective that patients are cured after a treatment course of 5 to 10 days. What's more, the rising cost of drug research, development, and distribution have combined with rising liability costs and narrow profit margins to make antimicrobial R&D a high-risk investment.

Nevertheless, I believe that Pfizer must keep working on the antibiotics of tomorrow. Even though we cannot solve the challenge of human illness on our own, we are willing to invest wholeheartedly in partnerships with government, private foundations, and United Nations agencies to increase basic access to health and healthcare. The only reason we can make these investments is because we can attract investment in a high-risk, high-reward business.[5]

We have perennial debates within Pfizer about where to focus our resources. Should we be putting resources into preparing to fight SARS or the next influenza pandemic, perhaps avian flu? Or should our focus be on resistant streptococcal pneumonia disease, which, if untreatable, is likely to kill more people over a 10-year period than an outbreak of flu? Given that there is probably no good way to set priorities in terms of threat, I would rank resistant microbes as the infectious disease problem most urgently in need of a solution.

Some people say that innovation is too important to be left to the pharmaceutical industry, that there's too much conflict of interest in mixing science and business. Others say we should abandon in-house discovery and simply outsource the science to the universities and the National Institutes of Health (NIH). I disagree. The sovereignty of consumers as expressed by a free market continues to represent our best hope of discovering and developing therapies and cures. If we segregated the science from the market, I don't believe we'd make as much progress in finding new medicines. We depend on science to make discoveries, engineering to make them work, and medical marketing to bring them to patients. Yes, that's sometimes a contentious mix that leads to duplication. But until we live in a world of unlimited resources, there will always be priorities, and no system known to date works better at innovatively ordering priorities than the market.

Vaccine Promises

A vaccine for malaria would save more lives than virtually any imaginable health expenditure. But there is no vaccine for malaria, and in the absence of some changes, there is unlikely to be one.

The problem is that no industry is likely to invest in complicated research projects if it has little reason to think it will recoup its costs much less show a return. And while there is exciting malaria research taking place in government labs and universities around the world, the chances of a for-profit organization taking the risk to turn the research into a real product are slim. As long as governments hold down vaccine prices, and most vaccines are sold to developing nations at pennies per dose, there are few economic incentives to develop vaccines.

Thirty years ago there were 25 private-sector companies—Pfizer was one of them—producing vaccines. But vaccine producers have abandoned the field in droves. Today there are only one or two suppliers for most of the many vaccines used to fight the major diseases affecting developed nations. Most exited the vaccine business as a consequence of relentless lawsuits filed on behalf of people alleging negative side effects to vaccines. The National Childhood Vaccine Injury Act of 1986 has been one response to create a no-fault compensation alternative to suing vaccine manufacturers and providers on behalf of people injured or killed by vaccines. Congress provided incentives for the production of safer vaccines by establishing a compensation program that helps prevent future vaccine injuries through education and an adverse reaction reporting system.[6]

There are even fewer vaccine options for diseases primarily affecting the developing countries. Of the 1233 drugs licensed worldwide between 1975 and 1997, only 13 were for tropical disease, and only four were developed by commercial drug makers specifically for human tropical diseases.[7] Industry needs a combination of "push" and "pull" market mechanisms to overcome the problems of developing vaccines, and especially vaccines for the developing world.

Incentive systems that encourage the development of new products can be categorized as *push* incentives. Examples of push incentives include subsidies and other inputs. The well-functioning market offers pull incentives in the form of profits for companies that introduce successful products and services. For example, consumers didn't ask for the photocopier machine, but Xerox took the risk that if it introduced the product to the market, it would find success.

I am excited about the dramatic announcement by Gordon Brown, Britain's Chancellor of the Exchequer, to commit his government, in cooperation with other partners, to call an AIDS or malaria vaccine into existence by guaranteeing a lucrative market to the first developer to hit a carefully specified medical mark. This kind of commitment attempts to shape the spending and R&D decisions of private companies by guaranteeing an advance market for the drug company that develops a vaccine.

Unfortunately, neither push nor pull incentives are in place to facilitate aggressive vaccine R&D. In the flu season of 2004-2005, Americans experienced the worst flu vaccine shortage in this country's history. The proximate cause of this particular shortage was the loss of half the required national supply from one of the two companies that manufactures flu vaccine. Unless we attend to the root cause of the problem, we can expect similar shortages from time to time in the supplies of vaccines used to prevent childhood diseases like mumps, measles, and diphtheria.

Ironically, vaccines fell victim to their own success. These are absolutely miracle drugs that have changed the world as much or more than any other technology. They were so successful that demand for vaccines prompted governments to become the major customer. The government's preoccupation with cost led to very low returns for vaccine manufacturers. At the same time, the high legal costs required to defend liability lawsuits doomed the nation's human vaccine research and development capability.

The law of high numbers seems to work against human vaccine makers. The diseases vaccines combat seem very remote, and the benefits they deliver seem slight. The reality, of course, is that every drug carries some risk. But because vaccines are given to large numbers of healthy people, safety and liability concerns can seem greater than with drugs that are given to sick people, who are willing to bear some risk of side effects to get better.

By this logic, when a drug's benefits clearly outweigh its risks—such as chemotherapy agents, which desperate patients accept as highly toxic—a drug is safe from jury verdicts. But when the benefits are perceived as slight and a patient has an adverse experience, then it becomes tempting for lawyers to make the case that the drug is, in essence, defective. Birth control drugs, for example, are very low risk but attract a huge amount of litigation because people have come to take the benefits for granted. It's the same for vaccines.

Pfizer is a poster child for the unintended consequences of vaccine policy in this country. Ironically, although we concluded that the company could not make a go of it in the human vaccine sector, Pfizer leads the world in animal health vaccine research and development. The difference between the two sectors could not be starker. Animals don't file lawsuits, and there is no single-source buyer for animal health vaccines.

To reverse this course, the government should take a number of measures. First, it should increase funding for basic research on subunit and conventional vaccines. Second, regulators should pursue agreements on reciprocity of approvals so that vaccines and antiretroviral drugs licensed in certain foreign counties can also be marketed in the United States and vice versa. Third, the policy of extracting huge discounts by the CDC, the major purchaser of vaccines in the United States, must be recognized as counterproductive. Finally, I call on Congress to improve the climate for vaccine manufacturers by limiting lawsuits for side effects of vaccines that have received FDA approval.

Drug Discovery Will Continue

As long as the incentives are in place, drug discovery will continue. Whether it will be successful in filling our medicine cabinets with the drugs we need to treat current and emerging threats to health is another matter. There are no guarantees. The search is progressing and so is the science. Every failure moves us closer to the light. I have confidence that the application of vast amounts of human intelligence, passion, money, and time is the recipe for eventual success.

When the setbacks come—and they come regularly—and the work of discovering the medicine to treat cancer, or diabetes, or asthma seems most futile, I recall something the novelist Henry James wrote about the discovery process: "We work in the dark—we do what we can—we give what we have. Our doubt is our passion, and our passion is our task."[8]

CHAPTER 11

INFORMATION INTENSIVE: REAPING THE BENEFITS OF TECHNOLOGY

"Mr. Jones, are you allergic to any medications?" It was 8:10 a.m., and it was the fifth time since checking in for his surgery earlier that morning that the patient was asked this question. As the anesthesia started to take effect, the patient wondered why everyone kept repeating the same question. Didn't they talk to each other?

Mr. Jones' surgery proceeded without complication. The trust that he had placed in his personal physician, his surgeon, and the nurses was well founded—at least on this day. But the inability of the doctors and nurses to consult integrated, real-time medical information delivered at the point of care exposed Mr. Jones to real risk. There was a reason the healthcare professionals kept repeating that question. Many of them had experience with inadvertently giving patients a medication to which they were allergic. What they did not have experience with is a health information system that would make such errors a thing of the past.

The fragmentation of the healthcare systems of the world injures people senselessly and unnecessarily, and it is preventable. Approximately 100,000 people in the United States die as the result of medical error—more than are killed by breast cancer.[1] When seven astronauts died in the Space Shuttle Columbia explosion in 2003, NASA grounded the Space Shuttle program and turned itself inside out to find the cause of the problem and to ensure it never happens again. When an airplane crashes, the National Transportation Safety Board swings into action to find the preventable errors and to correct them. Yet, although all healthcare professionals privately acknowledge a lamentable record of preventable medical error, there is little being done except hand-wringing and more studies. Why do we accept a system that does not value lives in hospitals as much as it values lives in space shuttles and airplanes?

One of the biggest obstacles to reducing preventable medical error is the fantasy that the problem is not really so deadly. Unfortunately, it is. Newt Gingrich, who after leaving the House of Representatives, has written widely on healthcare reform, tells the following story. At the end of a speech in which he quoted the figure of 100,000 preventable deaths per year due to medical error, a doctor in the audience angrily challenged him. "That statistic is widely inflated," the doctor yelled. "The true number is no more than 25,000." Gingrich let a few seconds go by and then responded, "Okay, you win."[2]

I'm convinced that technology, or more precisely, the lack of the right kind of information technology, is at the bottom of medical errors. The technology is out there. The banking and insurance industries have figured it all out. What's lacking in the healthcare system are the incentives and trust to put information to work on behalf of patients. Simply stated, there are at present few incentives for hospitals, doctors, nurses, and other healthcare professionals to get behind this technology. They are afraid that, if they do, the resulting information will be used against them. The latter point is a consequence of the adversarial, litigation-prone medical system we have evolved. Cost-shifting, fault-finding, and finger-pointing are not the best ground to plant the seeds of new technologies.

Other industries have figured out how to deliver services with decreasing numbers of errors. Think about all the Starbucks coffees you've ordered. Has Starbucks ever made a mistake? Everyone involved in healthcare delivery can learn a lot from Starbucks, which has particular systems in place to prevent mistakes. The next time you go in for a half-caf, half-decaf cappuccino with skim milk, notice how many employees repeat your order after you place it. Then look at the check marks on your cup made to back up the verbal order. This is teamwork and a well-designed system. The company has created a culture among its employees that embraces the system and quickly identifies errors.

Starbucks will eventually formalize the redundancy and "read-back" features of this process in a database-driven system initiated at point of sale. But for now the system works and has become part of the Starbucks experience.

Another source of lessons on improving healthcare safety is the aviation industry. Between 1967 and 1976, the risk of dying in a domestic jet flight was one in two million. By the 1990s, that risk fell to one in eight million. How did the aviation industry achieve this reduction? By designing information systems that automate and standardize many tasks and controls. The aviation industry also defines best practices (checklists) and employs "read-back" and other techniques to increase communication and teamwork.

Almost as important as the technology, the aviation industry has instilled a culture that emphasizes learning over blame. Pilots and other aviation workers are strongly encouraged to report errors and near misses without fear of recrimination. This is possible because the confidential Aviation Safety Reporting System (ASRS) is not under the jurisdiction of the Federal Aviation Administration, the agency that regulates the industry. Instead, ASRS is a part of NASA, which has no regulatory authority over the airlines. It is ASRS that collects the data and reviews the reports of "close calls" or near misses and issues alerts of different levels based on the seriousness of the situation. If the healthcare industry is serious about reducing medical errors, it will support the aggregation of quality data in an institution that is dedicated to eliminating blunders, not punishing blunderers.

The fact is, we really don't know how many deaths occur due to preventable medical error. Nor do we have reliable statistics on the errors that do not actually result in death. The best estimates suggest that out of every 100 hospital patients, five or six are the victims of preventable hospital error. In addition, from 5 to 10 percent of all hospital patients— two million people per year—contract a hospital-acquired infection. Remarkably, these infections are not considered medical errors and because they are not so labeled, we actually have *better* statistics for these incidents. The Institute of Medicine reports that preventable adverse patient events, including hospital-acquired infections, are responsible for 44,000-98,000 deaths annually at a cost of $17-$29 billion.[3]

Technology is not the problem, and it's not the solution. We have to overcome significant cultural barriers in medicine before we can give technology a chance to work. So before we wax enthusiastic about all the very real benefits that the Internet and information technology are poised to bring to medicine, we need to start dismantling these barriers. Let me give you a few examples of what I mean.

Mrs. Smith has asthma, a chronic condition that in many cases can be managed with medication. She is getting low on pills so she visits her doctor, who gives her a checkup, adjusts her dosage, and writes her a new prescription. Assume that the doctor is up-to-date and uses electronic prescribing, working with a handheld instrument like a personal digital assistant. Once the doctor taps in the patient's name and prescription, the information is transmitted directly to Mrs. Smith's preferred pharmacy, where it is filled and available for pickup. The primary purpose of issuing a prescription electronically, as opposed to the old paper pad, is reducing medical errors. These include errors caused by illegible handwriting, confusion about similar drug names, and misreading the dosage prescribed for the patient.

Doctors are sometimes surprised to learn that up to a third of the prescriptions they write are never filled. Sometimes the patient can't afford to pay for the prescription and is too embarrassed to tell the doctor. Sometimes the patient loses the prescription or just forgets to fill it. If the physician assumes the patient is actually taking the medication when they are not, the course of treatment might well be compromised.

With paper-based systems, there is no easy way for physicians to be notified if a particular prescription has not been filled. With electronic prescribing it becomes much easier. The technology is tested and ready to go. The tragedy is that cultural barriers—in this case, the lack of incentives and the perennial fear of malpractice litigation—block the closing of this medical error wormhole.

Doctors could have an enormous amount of information available to them, but they often don't want it. For example, most doctors would theoretically welcome knowing if a patient has not filled a prescription. But right now the system rewards ignorance and blesses a certain level of error. Here's why: If doctors are not aware of whether a patient has filled a prescription or not, they cannot be held responsible.

Suppose doctors are alerted to the fact that a patient has not filled a script. Do they then have a responsibility to telephone the patient? If they do, it will be on their own dime because there is no reimbursement for such calls. If they don't, and the patient gets worse, are doctors exposing themselves to liability? Right now, the electronic prescribing system is just one-way. A more expensive two-way communications system is required to enable the feedback that a prescription has or has not been filled. Who will pay for the incremental cost? Guess who would be stuck with the bill? It's hard to blame doctors for resisting the whole thing and sticking with paper prescriptions. And if a few patients get the wrong meds or the wrong dosage on occasion, well, that's the fault of the system.

Pharmacies have also been bit by cultural barriers. Suppose it's the pharmacist who notices that Mrs. Smith has not filled the prescription for the asthma meds. So what happens when the drugstore sends out a friendly reminder that the prescription is waiting to be filled? Mrs. Smith may complain that she is being subject to unwelcome marketing or intrusions on her privacy. What are the parameters defining personal autonomy and healthcare information?

Never Pay for "Nevers"

The medical system has a unique business model. The worse it treats you, the more money it gets. For years, the system has rewarded bad results: patients who get sicker require more procedures and, therefore, earn more money for physicians and hospitals. Medical errors are rife. Because it is almost impossible for patients to know the error rates for individual hospitals and doctors, there is little incentive for the providers to minimize mistakes.

Two quick changes would go a long way to solving the problem. The first step is to rigorously collect the error data and publish it. If we required every hospital to publish the number of dropped babies, surgeries on wrong body parts, wrong drugs or dosages, deaths from hospital-borne infections, etc., I guarantee you that hospitals would shape up overnight. The public overwhelmingly supports the right to know such quality data so they can make informed judgments about which hospital to select. What gets measured gets improved; what gets measured and reported publicly gets improved faster. When we make the errors public, the pressure on the worst hospitals to change would be almost instantaneous. It wouldn't require government action. The market would evolve information clearinghouses and "Good Housekeeping Seal of Approval" certification services. Let's collect the data, make all medical errors a matter of public record, and let the chips fall where they may.

The second step is to put healthcare professionals on notice that we will refuse to pay for preventable medical errors. You wouldn't pay for a botched car repair, so why would you pay for botched surgery? Shouldice Hospital is on the right path with its policy not to pay doctors when they have to redo a hernia operation. The decision to stop paying for adverse events takes the philosophy a step further. Healthcare professionals should never be paid for 27 specific preventable medical events as defined by the National Quality Forum, a think tank made up of a coalition of hospitals, health plans, employers, and government.[4] The medical profession should understand that there will never be cash flow in the healthcare system for events such as:

- Surgery performed on wrong body part
- Patient death or serious disability associated with medical error
- Wrong drug or wrong dose given to patient
- Retention of foreign object in patient after surgery
- Contaminated blood transfusion
- Infant discharge to wrong mother
- Stage 3 or 4 pressure ulcers

Insurance companies are just starting to take this position. HealthPartners, the third biggest health insurer in Minnesota, will no longer pay for certain procedures it calls "nevers." Saving money is not really the issue. These events are thankfully rare (which is not the same as never), so the cost savings won't add up to much, but HealthPartners thinks it's about quality and accountability. The firm is sending a message that providers who make certain mistakes should not expect to be paid for them.

Decision Support and Decision Control

Healthcare professionals require outcomes-based information to provide the best diagnosis, treatment, and results. They want real-time information: knowledge that reaches the practitioner and the patient as rapidly and accurately as possible, delivering it with privacy and security at the lowest overall cost. The good news is that the explosion in the capabilities of computers and communications makes it possible for every patient and every case to be part of a worldwide system of best outcomes, best solutions, and most recent knowledge and innovation in a manner literally impossible even 10 years ago.

But building the system to deliver these outcomes is not easy. Doctors have been burned by early experiments in eHealth. To their dismay, they have found that systems that promised to give them decision support (tools to increase autonomy and make decisions smarter, faster, and easier) frequently delivered decision control (limiting autonomy and coercively attempting to control the decision to a predetermined set of outcomes).

The truth is that information technology is both a bane and a salvation. It can create new vistas for medical quality, clinical outcomes, and innovation. And medical information systems can be hijacked by special interests; they can be biased inadvertently or by design.

The lesson is that everyone has an agenda. That's not necessarily bad. Progress occurs when the agendas of many different players compete for success on a level playing field. Agendas become destructive when they are hidden. And that's what makes information technology especially vulnerable. It's too easy to hide biases and agendas within the "black boxes" that form the core of all systems.

For example, electronic prescribing or eRx is a lifesaving technology that has been widely deployed in institutional settings. Many health plans require their participating physicians to prescribe electronically. Yet despite its clear advantages, many physicians in outpatient settings have resisted eRx. We saw one reason for this resistance earlier in the chapter—liability from junk lawsuits—but unfortunately there are others.

Some physicians are mistrustful of eRx. Their fears tend to run along two dimensions. First, they believe that the algorithms embedded within the system might limit their autonomy by the choices the system makes available. For example, let's go back to the example of Mrs. Smith. After giving her a medical exam, the doctor punches in her symptom with the intent to prescribe a medication that his experience tells him is most appropriate. The doctor looks at the list of medications for that symptom, but the system does not list the preferred medication. Why is it not there? Did the sponsors of the system leave it off because it is too expensive? Are they giving other drugs preferred positions? Now the doctor has to jump through another hoop to prescribe the drug or accept one of the convenient choices. The doctor is concerned that the order-of-medication list might be driven not by medical concerns for the patient, but because some third party may benefit financially.

The second reason for mistrust is that doctors are fearful that the statistics collected by these systems will be used against them. Given the lack of trust, it will be hard to persuade the physician community that these systems will not be used against them in a disciplinary way. We need to build the bridges to get clinicians to believe these systems are being deployed to benefit patients, not to discipline clinicians.

"I would actually like to know if my prescribing habits and my patients' outcomes differ substantially from my colleagues," a rheumatologist practicing in the New York area told me. Like most doctors he is intensely interested in outcomes and learning different approaches and techniques. The information systems we are talking about would give doctors this knowledge, which they could then consider incorporating into their practices. In this way, good ideas get adopted and clinical outcomes improve. But overshadowing the benefit to them and their practices is the fear that such information will be used against them.

There is one condition absolutely essential for the rapid dissemination of ideas in a community. The members must be forthright about their mistakes. This condition is almost completely absent in

American medicine today. "I'm terrified about admitting mistakes," the surgeon told me, "because I'm at the mercy of my medical malpractice insurance carrier who looks for the slightest excuse to raise rates or drop my coverage altogether." This attitude puts a big roadblock in the adoption curve for innovation in medicine. We've moved to a model of care where everyone is looking over everyone else's shoulder to find fault. From my own experience as a manager, I can tell you that a punitive approach is exactly the wrong way to promote quality and innovation.

Despite these considerable obstacles, if we want healthcare to aspire to the best that we can hope for instead of the minimum that we want to spend, there is no alternative to putting our reliance on information systems. Metrics are the way to make things happen. I'm not just talking about the truism that you can't manage what you can't measure. I'm talking about collecting data on every aspect of the healthcare delivery system and, here's the kicker, making the data public. There is no better way to minimize waste and corruption, promote innovation, and keep people honest than to shine a bright light on the proceedings.

Physicians in the United States will resist every attempt to create electronic records, however it might benefit them, if they have the slightest worry that the contents of those records will be used against them by medical malpractice lawyers. The trouble is, it's virtually impossible to craft an information-rich, integrated electronic medical records system that does not make physicians more accountable. Indeed, that's one of the main objectives of the system. We need to have physicians, like other professionals, accountable for the consequences of their behavior. The goal is to put accountability in the service of improving quality and rectifying defects, not shifting costs or blame.

Yet we mustn't allow ourselves to be seduced by technology because, like healthcare itself, there is a very inequitable spread in how technology is distributed. Some developments are transformative. More and more of the work of researchers is moving from the chemistry lab to the computer lab. Information technology builds on itself in the sense that the Internet and the PC are themselves tools to create more innovation. Yet most people in the world continue to live in very poor conditions, and our ability to focus innovation on the things that would save lives is limited. People living in developed countries have iPods and cell phones with distinctive ring tones. But are we really making the advances to improve human conditions where most people live? We can—and must—do better.

CHAPTER 12

CHANGE IS POSSIBLE: INFECTIOUS DISEASE AND THE STRUGGLE FOR HOPE

When it comes to global health, it's easy to be a pessimist. From the pandemic of HIV/AIDS, malaria, and tuberculosis in sub-Saharan Africa to the rise of diabetes and asthma in developing nations, the problems are overwhelming. It's easy to lose heart. The Yiddish writer Isaac Bashevis Singer observed, "If you keep saying that things are going to be bad, you have a good chance of becoming a prophet."[1] I'm not interested in prophets that divine hopelessness; tomorrow is up to each of us to shape, one way or the other.

In this book, I have tried to take a no-excuses attitude to making this a healthier world for us and our children. I believe it is much better to try and fail than to not try at all. Here, I describe the major humanitarian initiatives that give me hope, even in the face of heartbreaking misery. Some of these projects have worked better than others, and I have learned much along the way. My point is not that these were the best projects we could have taken on or that we executed them flawlessly—in fact we made lots of mistakes. My point is that none of us has complete information and yet it's on such incomplete, occasionally conflicting information that we must act.

Hope emerges from small decisions made powerful by persistence and patience. Very early in my career, I learned something about both. In 1974, just one year after I joined Pfizer, I was preparing to take on the responsibility of being a country manager in Iran. On a dusty

Middle Eastern morning, my family and I arrived in this beautiful and troubled land filled with the most generous people on earth.

The manager of the Pfizer manufacturing operation in Iran met my wife and me along with our three daughters, Alison, Tracy, and Karin, at the airport. Our home in Tehran would not be ready for some days, so we went straight to the Hilton. The next morning, the country manager I was replacing drove me to the Pfizer administrative office. It was next to the manufacturing plant that made a variety of Pfizer products for Iran, Afghanistan, and surrounding markets.

As we drove into the complex, I saw a line of about 25 anxious-looking men waiting at the gate. Later that day, the plant manager explained that they were day laborers who walked out to the plant at dawn to wait for the possibility of work of any kind. Often they waited the entire day without being called, and then, with empty pockets, they trudged back home. When a man was selected, the pay was 10 Iranian rials per day, equivalent to about $1.50 in the United States.[2]

The situation did not sit well with me. It was neither an effective way of using day labor nor a dignified way to treat workers. And the pay seemed unconscionably low. But I was the new kid on the block and everyone assured me that the arrangement was unremarkable in Iran. "The men are used to it," was the message I got. "This is the way it's done in Iran, and we've been doing it this way forever." I have never accepted this philosophy. It seems to me that the advantage of rotating managers from country to country is to promote the transfer of best practices, spur innovation, and increase accountability. Tradition, of course, has a vote, but not a veto. It seemed to me even then that holding out high standards—in this case, treating workers with respect and care—was the right thing to do. This principle has only become more important to me over time.

It took years, but we did improve conditions for day laborers. Four years later, when I left the Tehran plant for the last time, my car entered the Pfizer gate at the same time a bus filled with workers arrived. They did not pay me any attention, nor should they have. Their minds were focused on making a day's wage for a day's labor so they could feed their families. These were the laborers who for that day, at least, would contribute their skills to making Pfizer successful. I thought the least we could do was to send a bus to a designated spot in Tehran each day to pick up the laborers we needed. The rate by then was 100 rials per day (about $13 in the United States). We also provided the workers with the same midday meal that I ate each day, and drove them back to Tehran at the end of their shift. I'm sure some of my colleagues in Iran saw it as the excesses of a soft-headed Westerner. But I saw it as economic development. Economic development, like healthcare, starts by empowering one human being at a time.

So the lot of a few day laborers in Tehran improved. A big deal? Not really, I suppose, in the sweep of history that was about to engulf Iran. But I like to think that the Iranians we treated well put just a little more of themselves into their work and perhaps thought just a little better of Americans.

Political turmoil was in the air. My family and I departed Iran in 1977. In January 1979, the Shah of Iran and his family were forced into exile. The Islamic fundamentalist Ayatollah Khomeini returned to Iran from exile in France and the Islamic Republic of Iran was proclaimed in April. On November 4th, Islamic militants took 52 Americans hostage inside the U.S. embassy in Tehran. Of the militants, I prefer to think that, whatever their backgrounds and motivations, none of them ever spent time on the Pfizer bus.

The Infrastructure of Hope

As the sun rose in the sky, I coveted the stylish hat that Ugandan President Yoweri Museveni wore. In the unforgiving noontime sun of Kampala, I myself was hatless. What can I say? I am not in the custom of wearing hats in October. But the equatorial sun did not diminish my contentment. This was a day of triumph.

The occasion was the dedication of the Infectious Disease Institute (IDI), a state-of-the-art clinical care facility that today is training healthcare workers, providing treatment to people living with HIV/AIDS, conducting research to strengthen protocols of care, and supporting prevention programs. It is the first significant addition in 40 years to the campus of Makerere University in Kampala, Uganda, and, as far as I can tell, it has no equal in Africa.

Rarely have I felt so hopeful. Five years in the making, the IDI is providing comprehensive outpatient AIDS treatment to Ugandans who are already infected and delivering critical education services to prevent future infections. As a clinical facility, it accommodates 200 adult and pediatric patients per day, or about 50,000 patient visits per year. As a training facility, the IDI has already graduated hundreds of students, healthcare providers from Uganda, and more than a dozen other countries throughout Africa. The facility is the product of a public partnership between the Academic Alliance for AIDS Care and Prevention in Africa, Pfizer, and Makerere University.

On the day we dedicated the IDI, I accepted that what we celebrated was a milestone, not a finish line. The finish line is the end of AIDS on earth. That's many years and too many lives away. But because talented people put their hearts and minds together in one shared vision to make the world measurably healthier, that finish line is just a bit closer.

Social Investment

At most Pfizer annual meetings, I am asked why the company spends so much money on humanitarian efforts and other social investment activities. It's a reasonable question. A case can be made that the business of enterprises is to pay maximum returns to shareholders who are better positioned to decide which humanitarian efforts are worthy of support.

My view is different. I believe that Pfizer has an obligation to the communities in which we operate. Those who welcome us into their communities can expect social investment. Pfizer is a global company with 115,000 employees who live and work in more than 100 countries. What connects us is our shared values and vision of what it means to be a responsible company in today's world. Social investment at Pfizer is not a program. It isn't a list of projects. Social investment is nothing less than the way we do business responsibly, one opportunity, one community, one challenge at a time.

In the late 1990s, the politics surrounding the HIV/AIDS epidemic in sub-Saharan Africa had the potential to undermine the ability of the pharmaceutical industry to function. The industry was increasingly being perceived as part of the problem instead of as part of the solution. I believed that what was at risk was nothing less than the fundamental compact that allows pharmaceutical companies like Pfizer to operate.

Pfizer was being attacked by AIDS activists and others for obstructing the flow of HIV/AIDS medicines to developing countries. The critics charged that it was our patents and high prices that spelled the deaths of millions of people in sub-Saharan Africa. I felt the ground under Pfizer begin to shift. Never mind that the charges had no basis in fact. If society perceives our organization as a problem, we'll be treated as a problem. If society perceives our organization as part of the solution, we'll be treated as a partner in that solution.

The relentless criticism threatened our bargain with society. Under this bargain, the industry makes enormous investments to develop important medicines to benefit society. In exchange, society gives us a certain period of time through the patent system to earn a return on that investment. Given the deteriorating situation in sub-Saharan Africa and the ferocity of the attacks against us, I saw pressures mounting to dismantle patent rights and the other incentives, including our ability to reward investors, on which our success hinges.

Social investment is movement toward a value proposition that makes pharmaceutical innovation possible. Strong intellectual property protection and market-based pricing of medicines in developed countries allow us to earn the returns that fund our programs to help patients in less-developed regions.

From Cost to Compassion: The Public Health Crisis of Our Generation

Unless the world gets its priorities straight, HIV/AIDS will become the most catastrophic human disease in history. It is more destructive than the bubonic plague, which, known as the Black Death, killed more than a quarter of the population in Europe in the fourteenth century. It is worse than cholera; more dangerous than tuberculosis, with which it is frequently associated; worse than smallpox, which thankfully has been eradicated after killing untold millions of people. HIV/AIDS is worse, in fact, than the Spanish flu epidemic of 1918, which killed at least 25 million people in one year. The HIV/AIDS pandemic is a threat to each of us, unlike any other disease in history.

In the developed world, HIV infection is no longer a death sentence. For many infected people lucky to have access to modern medications, HIV infection is a manageable chronic infection. A sense of triumph is well deserved, but the advance will be a poor bargain if it breeds a false sense of complacency among the leaders of the world and the world's at-risk popultions. In sub-Saharan Africa, and increasingly in India, Russia, and elsewhere, HIV/AIDS is largely uncontrolled.

Africa has three-quarters of the world's HIV/AIDS burden. There the overwhelming and pitiful consequences of the disease play out for all who have the courage to witness it. Across the continent, AIDS has reduced life expectancy to levels not seen since the 1800s, erasing the hard-won economic gains that many African nations have made in the last 25 years. "It is the most efficient impoverishing agent you can find; it just sucks out the resources," says Dr. Derek von Wissell, director of Swaziland's National Emergency Response Council on HIV/AIDS.[3] The situation in the next 10 years is spreading to Asia and Russia.

Unlike most of the great plagues in history, HIV doesn't just kill the young and vulnerable. It hollows out centers of societies by killing the most vital people. So in Swaziland, Botswana, South Africa, and elsewhere, societies are losing half their teachers, half their healthcare workers, half their police and military officers. Many villages are now populated by AIDS orphans without adult supervision. What will become of these children? Raised without moral guidance, analysts fear they will be ripe for recruiting by terrorists. Not without reason is HIV/AIDS the first disease to be labeled a global security threat by the United Nations Security Council.

Collaborative Efforts

What contributes most to the effectiveness of humanitarian programs are the collaborative efforts to build local infrastructure and capacity so that products and services reach those who need them. I realized that in 1995 Pfizer didn't have the technical competencies or partnerships in place to implement successfully a major HIV/AIDS humanitarian initiative. Drugs aren't like food aid; you don't just throw pills off the back of a truck. People need to be diagnosed, and they need to be monitored. The distribution of drugs needs to be secure against diversion. What's needed is an infrastructure that often has to be created from scratch. We decided to launch two focused efforts that would pave the way for something more comprehensive.

Two products in Pfizer's drug portfolio are particularly relevant to address significant health threats in Africa. We decided to learn about working in Africa by donating these products as part of a comprehensive program attacking the problem. The first partnership combats trachoma, an easily transmittable eye infection that victimizes children and women and is the leading cause of preventable blindness. The second partnership distributes a very effective medicine for treating the opportunistic fungal infections that often debilitate people with AIDS.

I saw how doctors combated trachoma in Iran 30 years ago, and how they were limited by the medicines they had available. The conventional treatment at the time was an antibiotic ointment applied to the eye three times a day for six weeks. As a result, compliance suffered and many interventions failed. More recently, we learned that a single oral dose of Pfizer's Zithromax antibiotic has a much better cure rate. We launched a program to donate our antibiotic to people in need. In 1998, with the Edna McConnell Clark Foundation and the World Health Organization, we created the International Trachoma Initiative. The goal: use simple surgery, better sanitation, improved patient information, and the Zithromax treatment to wipe out the disease by 2020.

We continue to treat active infections by donating Zithromax, and the International Trachoma Initiative demonstrates that while an effective medication isn't the whole answer, it is part of the answer. Today the ITI operates in Ghana, Egypt, Mali, Morocco, Niger, Sudan, Tanzania, Vietnam, and Nepal. More than five million people have been cured of active trachoma infection. The World Health Organization's goal of eliminating this leading cause of preventable blindness by 2020 is on track. We went from treating a few kids in a few villages to eradicating a major scourge of the developing world.

Using what Pfizer learned from the trachoma project, we were ready to join the battle against HIV/AIDS. In 2000, we started the Diflucan Partnership Program in South Africa, one of the nations hardest hit by AIDS. Diflucan is an antifungal medicine highly effective for the treatment of two serious opportunistic fungal infections associated with HIV/AIDS.[4]

Since its inception, Pfizer has trained more than 20,000 healthcare professionals and donated more than four million doses of Diflucan to participating institutions operating at 915 sites in 21 African countries, from Botswana to Zimbabwe. So successful is the program that Pfizer has expanded the eligibility criteria of the Diflucan program to include all developing countries with an HIV/AIDS infection rate of more than 1 percent. Pfizer operates the Diflucan Partnership in 18 African countries, as well as Haiti, Cambodia, and Honduras.

Rehearsal for Something Bigger

As important as the trachoma and Diflucan initiatives are, they are by nature reactive. I knew that they were a rehearsal for something even bigger, a project that attacked HIV at its source, a project that focused on prevention, and one that could make a permanent difference to a large number of people.

I remember my initial meeting with Ugandan President Yoweri Museveni. In 1986, he seized a nation devastated by endless war and set about transforming it into an African success story. Former U.S. Secretary of State Madeleine Albright called him a "beacon of hope" for Africa, part of a new generation of leaders committed to solving the continent's problems. He privatized failing state industries and brought runaway inflation under control. His administration doubled the number of children in primary school, gave women a guaranteed share of political seats, and stemmed a threatened AIDS epidemic.

The big problem with getting leaders in Africa to champion HIV prevention efforts is that many leaders don't see how they can succeed.

Politicians, and not only in Africa, are reluctant to expend political capital on causes they are not sure they can win. Unlike many African leaders, President Museveni was willing to take the heat for getting a project like the IDI built. He understood that for his country to reverse its rising infection rate, the personal behavior of its citizens would have to be challenged through education and prevention programs.

In the beginning, we had many discussions about the scope of our partnership in Uganda. President Museveni suggested that what Uganda needed most was infrastructure to train health professionals. This seemed correct to me, and we considered a number of possibilities. When the subject of Makerere University came up, I was particularly intrigued. Established by the British in 1922, Makerere University was the first modern university in East Africa and soon attracted the best students from the continent. Its medical school was especially renowned. However, during the brutal regime of Idi Amin, the university, like many of Uganda's institutions, fell on hard times. Soldiers looted the library and killed the school's top administrators. When I learned that many of the medical school's top faculty members had returned to Uganda, I knew we had found an opportunity.

Former U.S. President Jimmy Carter helped me decide that Uganda was the place for Pfizer to begin making a proactive impact in sub-Saharan Africa. At a time when HIV/AIDS was ravaging the continent, Uganda achieved an extraordinary feat: it stopped the spread of HIV/AIDS in its tracks and lowered the infection rate by two-thirds. The "Uganda Miracle" did not require big investments in high technology. The effort focused on grass-roots prevention, education, and behavior modification. Mostly, it succeeded because of the willingness of the Ugandan president and the first lady to tell the truth. It was a level of candor unprecedented in sub-Saharan Africa. And as we saw more recently in the SARS outbreak in China, the lack of candor by public health officials in dealing forthrightly with health crises is still a concern with potential fatal consequences.

President Museveni wasted no time in launching a blunt education campaign about the deadliness of the disease and the hazards of irresponsible sexual activity. Within a year of taking office in 1986, he had articulated a three-pronged strategy to prevent new infections. For the majority of people, the emphasis was on monogamy. The emphasis for youth was on abstinence. Condoms were offered as a last resort, mostly for high-risk groups. The message was delivered from middle-school classrooms to churches to community seminars and in radio, print, and television broadcasts. The government established highly effective partnerships with the religious community. The effect was to create a "social vaccine" against HIV, leveraging the reality that HIV infection is 100 percent preventable.

In Uganda, the "ABC approach" to HIV/AIDS prevention proved its effectiveness. ABC is shorthand for the three important elements of the program: Abstain, Be faithful, use Condoms. ABC refers to individual behaviors, but it also refers to the program approach and content designed to encourage those behaviors. The effectiveness of the program in Uganda is undisputed. The U.S. Census Bureau/UNAIDS estimates that Ugandan HIV prevalence peaked at about 15 percent in 1991 and fell to 5 percent as of 2001.[5]

All three elements of the program are vital. All three are also lightning rods for ideological agendas by governments and others. It distresses me that despite the scientific evidence, many still want prevention policy focused on promoting the first element of the program and de-emphasizing the third. U.S. law requires that at least one-third of all U.S. assistance to prevent HIV/AIDS globally be reserved for abstinence-until-marriage programs; this strikes me as unrealistic.

Correct and consistent use of condoms is an essential element of an effective risk-reduction tactic in the war on HIV. Conservatives attack condom distribution programs—like needle distribution programs—on the grounds that they legitimize promiscuity, prostitution, and illegal drug use. Conservatives believe that the availability of condoms has a "disinhibiting" effect on people's sexual behavior. Conservatives tend to favor a strict risk-elimination approach—which itself must be regarded as a risky strategy, given that risk elimination depends on 100 percent compliance 100 percent of the time.

We must all face the fact that HIV has evolved to exploit the way people actually behave, not the way we might want people to behave. If we need to debate issues of ideology in matters of public health, let us take care to debate them on our own time. We need to wage war on a virus, not on each other. HIV won't wait.

Three Conditions

I have learned a lot from the trachoma and Diflucan programs. The IDI has demonstrated that Pfizer could be a global partner in effective programs to fight disease and improve public health in the developing world. I've met with many heads of state who have requested Pfizer's help. I always respond by stating three conditions that need to be satisfied before we engage.

My first condition is getting an assurance that if there is a major impediment to the program, the head of state will take my call and will personally intercede to solve the problem. In six years, I've had to pick up the phone twice, once to South Africa and once to Uganda. In the case of South Africa, we couldn't ship Diflucan because we needed an approval for the package information insert from the ministry of health. After waiting three months, I phoned President Thabo Mbeki. A week later we had the approval.

I called Uganda because of a product diversion issue. The Diflucan we donated was turning up in the private market. So I put in a call to President Museveni and explained the situation. The next morning, the newspapers in Kampala carried a front page story featuring photos of a dozen or so pharmacists, all in handcuffs, looking very surprised. The diversion stopped.

The second condition is that we will not pay import duties. I understand that most African countries do not have an income tax, so they rely on import duties for much of their revenue. But I do not believe it is equitable to require pharmaceutical companies to pay 30 percent for the privilege of donating their products. So I tell the head of state that we'll donate the medications, but we won't pay import duties. I need true partners in these efforts.

The third condition is the one that's made some heads of state squirm. I tell them that if we start a program and that program is failing because of diversion of product by corrupt officials for their own profit, I will shut the program down and I will tell the world specifically why I shut it down. South Africa's President Mbeki was fine with that. "You're doing my job for me," he told me.

Unexpected Outcomes

All the outcomes I expected the IDI to deliver—the clinical treatment, the training, the prevention, the transfer of knowledge—are rolling out on schedule. But there are a number of things I didn't expect, and now these seem as important as the stated aims.

From the beginning, our determination to build the IDI to Western building standards met with resistance. Construction safety is not widely practiced in Uganda, so our insistence on a proper safety program, site safety, and incorporation of a building fire sprinkler system raised protests. I heard all kinds of objections, but the subtext was that lower standards for Africa were okay.

It wasn't okay with me. I didn't accept that argument in Iran at the beginning of my career, and I didn't accept it three decades later in Uganda. An attitude that calls for one set of standards for the developed world and a lower set of standards for the developing world is arrogant, condescending, and self-defeating. At best, the attitude is bad management: you end up spending more money than what it would cost to do it right. At worst, it's racist and perpetuates a miserable status quo. If you want the best from people, expect the best.

The standard for construction safety in Europe is one reportable accident for every 25,000 labor hours. We were told that it was unreasonable to expect Ugandan construction workers to work to such a standard. Nevertheless, we instituted a comprehensive safety program. Because personal protection equipment is such a critically important part of site safety, and most Ugandan workers do not own such equipment, we supplied every worker with hard hats, safety shoes, green jumpsuits, and high-visibility vests.

I didn't ask what number of construction accidents would have been considered acceptable for these workers, but I said that my goal for injured construction workers was zero (the same number as our goal for new HIV/AIDS infections). I believe that what you ask for is what you get. If you set lower standards, you'll get lower results in Africa or anywhere else.

One of the benefits of foreign and private investment is that it transfers best practices in ways you can't anticipate. I'm happy to report that we've operated at safety levels that would be enviable in the United States, and the construction workers in Uganda delivered it. We completed 250,000 labor hours without a significant accident and only five first-aid incidents.

It means a lot to me that we not only built the first new addition to the Makarere University campus since 1965, but we did so to best practice standards. I remember that at first President Museveni questioned the need for a fire sprinkler system. Now fire safety has become standard for new buildings in Uganda. Our site safety standards raised the bar for contractors throughout the construction trades in Kampala. Today, workers don't want to work without hard hats and safety shoes.

While the IDI was built to Western construction standards, in design it is uniquely Ugandan. The IDI avoids the centrally planned, high-tech approaches to public health that fail to meet the needs of the citizens. One mandate of the IDI is to train the trainers, who can then go to local villages and make allies with local traditional healers. These healers, among the most respected people in the communities, are an important resource in the battle against HIV. In Uganda, there is one medical doctor for every 10,000 people. But there is one traditional healer for every 150 people. Sure, we need to train more medical doctors, but if we can find a way to incorporate the support of traditional healers, that will make a big difference.

The IDI is equipped with all the resources of the latest HIV research lab in the developed world. We intend for the IDI to strike at the core of the AIDS epidemic by providing enhanced HIV care for adults, children, and families, including antiretrovirals and treatment for opportunistic infections. The IDI also conducts crucial research, not in the sense of discovering new drugs, but by monitoring the effectiveness of treatment regimens and identifying best practices for simple diagnoses.

One research project underway is to streamline diagnostic strategies. In the West we diagnose HIV through centralized laboratory systems that measure CD4 blood counts and viral loads. It's an approach that is expensive and requires high up-front investment, a combination of attributes unworkable in developing countries. Some researchers at the IDI believe that doctors can reliably monitor the progression of HIV treatment with little more than a thermometer and a bathroom scale. If patients are not running a fever and not losing weight, they are probably okay on their treatment regime. If they lose weight and their fever spikes, treatment is probably failing.

The Action Is More Important than the Call

Here's what I know about calls to action. The action is more important than the call. Motives count, but not as much as putting one foot in front of the other. My recognition that we needed to be part of the solution in combating the HIV epidemic in Africa came out of a mix of motives. Certainly, anyone who visits an orphanage in Africa comes back transformed. I remember sitting with a dozen small children in the infectious disease clinic in Uganda. All of them happy, young people who should have had bright futures ahead of them, except they all were HIV-positive and probably wouldn't live to be teenagers.

I thought about my granddaughter, Sarah, and the other grandchildren I hope to know. My vision is that someday during Sarah's life, she will witness the birth of children entering an HIV-free world. And it struck me that we have a choice. The choice is between sending our children to developing nations as emissaries of health and peace or sending our children to developing nations as soldiers to preserve security in the face of collapsing societies. This reality is devastating.

Hopeful Resolve

History is always testing our resolve. I believe future historians will see the worldwide HIV pandemic as the defining challenge of our time. Just like the children of my generation asked their parents what they did in the war against Nazi tyranny, our children will ask us what we did in the fight against the HIV threat. What will we be able to tell them?

The enormous scale of the AIDS pandemic and other scourges can cause one to lose hope. Yet, as I have learned firsthand in visiting some of the hardest-hit regions in Africa, hope exists in each person heroically battling the disease; in each new training center; in the blossoming of new partnerships that are engaging many different groups, measuring results, and taking responsibility to produce change; and in America's pledge to provide billions of dollars in assistance to fight AIDS in developing countries.

We have made some progress, but there is more to be done. Our people now have the tools, the experience, and the relationships with public and private institutions around the world to be effective partners where the need is greatest. Whether the need is chronic, as it is in Africa, or cataclysmic, as with the recent earthquake and tsunami in Southeast Asia, Pfizer is ready to do its part.

These efforts are bringing real care to patients who see us as their last best hope. To the extent we succeed, these efforts also are eroding the mind-set that says, "It's hopeless. Nothing can be done." And that is hopeful, indeed.

CHAPTER 13

NEXT STEPS: A CALL TO ACTION STARTS HERE

Throughout this book, I have identified concrete actions that I believe will move us closer to a world in which healthcare is seen as an investment to be valued rather than as a cost to be avoided. In this chapter, I bring these actions together in one place for further discussion. To my mind, these actions do not rise to the level of a coordinated program. It is not for an individual, nor a group of elites, to determine the course of the health of the world. If it is to be accepted, such a program will emerge from a sprawling partnership that brings together many parties in a spirit of candor, cooperation, and sacrifice. I see these actions as the components of what I hope will emerge as a social contract for delivering healthcare in the twenty-first century. It's now time to begin the discussion which will lead to meaningful action.

Reforming the healthcare system is a daunting challenge. The actions outlined in this book are some of the stepping stones I believe we will need to visit. There is much here to occupy us, and the unavoidable question is how do we prioritize? I start by suggesting 10 actions that I believe are a minimal list of reforms that will be required if healthcare is to rise to the standards that people deserve.

Ten Calls to Action

Throughout this book, I have indicated what I am prepared to do. Other calls to action must be implemented on an industrywide, regional, national, or even international level. Change at every level is needed to bring about the transformation we need. I believe the following actions are measurable, actionable, and achievable. They are all essential to a well-functioning healthcare system. The descriptions of these actions are necessarily brief because the details will have to emerge by consensus. I certainly don't have all the answers. I present them in the order they come up in this book.

1. Take Personal Responsibility for Your Health
2. Transform Employee Healthcare Plans
3. Adopt Specialized Medical Courts to Replace the Healthcare Liability System
4. Reform Direct-to-Consumer Advertising
5. Build a Level Playing Field for Health Savings Accounts
6. Use Trade Agreements to End "Free-Riding"
7. Maintain Incentives for Innovation
8. Demand Electronic Medical Records
9. Report on Corporate Citizenship
10. Initiate a Global Health Corps

One: Take Personal Responsibility for Your Health

I want to be very clear about what I mean by "personal responsibility" because the term has been hijacked by those motivated by self-interest in preserving the status quo. When we are asked to take more "personal responsibility," it is often code for shifting costs to the consumer, whether in the form of higher copays, larger deductibles, or reduced health coverage. This is definitely not what I mean by personal responsibility.

Taking personal responsibility means taking charge of our lives, challenging those individual behaviors that are not in the service of our long-term health and wellness. Most of us know what those behaviors are, and if we don't, the first call to action is to educate ourselves. Another action under the personal responsibility umbrella is "Know your numbers." That means taking steps to monitor our vital health statistics: blood pressure, cholesterol levels, weight, body mass index, HIV status, PSA levels (for men), and other relevant numbers.

We can no longer be passive recipients of healthcare services dispensed by faceless third parties. Each adult must accept full responsibility for funding and consuming healthcare services. Patriarchy, whether found in the workplace or doctor's office, must be replaced by a partnership. This is healthcare empowerment, and its benefits will create better lives for all of us.

Your First Move: Cardiovascular Health

Some calls to action for better health are simpler than others. Here's one that can be implemented right away. The benefits are unmistakable. It's free and there's no need to get anyone's permission. I call for each one of us to take charge of our cardiovascular health through three simple steps.

Taking charge of one's cardiovascular health starts with three steps. Each step should be taken in conjunction with your physician.

1. Know your numbers. That means periodically checking your blood pressure, cholesterol levels, and weight. Know your body mass index, resting heart rate, and heart rate recovery. As long as you're measuring, do you know your waist size?[1]
2. If you smoke, stop.
3. Exercise. Walking is the ideal exercise. Current guidelines recommend 30-60 minutes of moderate exercise per day. Walk 10,000 steps per day for long-term health and reduced chronic disease risk. Use a pedometer to measure your daily steps. If you currently average less than 10,000 steps, try increasing your average by 500 per day. For successful sustained weight loss, walk 12,000 to 15,000 steps per day. To build aerobic fitness, take 3,000 or more of your daily steps at a brisk pace.

Many of us are in cardiovascular denial. Fifty-seven percent do not believe they're at "much risk" for cardiovascular disease, and 59 percent do not believe it's our number-one killer, even though the disease is responsible for 40 percent of all mortality and the majority of morbidity and disability in the United States.[2]

There are few surprises in new dietary guidelines developed by the Department of Health and Human Services and the Agriculture Department. The guidelines call for Americans to lower their intake of calories, carbohydrates, fats, refined products, and salt. Recommended foods are fiber-rich vegetables and fruits and whole grains.

Heart disease and stroke, among the nation's leading causes of death and major causes of disability, are largely preventable. The simplest and most direct response to these health challenges starts with prevention as the first step. The savings in lives and money—cardiovascular disease costs Americans over $350 billion every year—are staggering.[3] Please join me in demonstrating that individual initiative can take a real dent out of the costs of cardiovascular disease. The health we gain is our own.

Two: Transform Employee Healthcare

If you're really worried about the high cost of disease, you become concerned about changing patient behaviors: things like the epidemic of obesity, diet, exercise, and early detection of disease. With the baby boom generation now moving into their 50s and 60s, we just can't afford to treat people at the level that will be required without fundamental changes in the system. We must keep the focus on prevention and wellness.

At Pfizer, we've begun an initiative to do just that. How can we tell governments that they need to do healthcare differently if we're not leaders in our own company? As we did in *Florida: A Healthy State*, we're beginning to implement a health-management program at Pfizer, so that we can assist colleagues with diabetes, heart disease, and other chronic conditions to better manage their overall health and improve their own outcomes.

I call on every organization to take a close look at the model they use for employee healthcare. The ideal model will promote the following outcomes:

- Encourage prevention and wellness
- Help patients manage their disease/conditions
- Reduce health disparities
- Support medical liability reform
- Manage out-of-pocket costs
- Increase access to insurance
- Increased use of technology to improve patient record sharing and overall system efficiency and effectiveness

To my regret, I came too late to the realization that Pfizer's employee healthcare program needed to be managed with the same diligence we brought to bear on R&D, marketing, manufacturing, and every other company function. It was easy to delegate this management challenge and not ask the tough questions about how much it's costing or how much value it is delivering. The problem is further compounded because most companies, ours included, promptly outsourced much of the task of employee healthcare to outside partners. We are now fully engaged with transforming employee healthcare. I call on business leaders to seize control of their employee healthcare destiny. I believe doing so is a moral imperative. I also think there is an untapped opportunity for organizations to seize competitive advantage by creative management of employee health.

Three: Adopt Specialized Medical Courts to Replace the Healthcare Liability System

The system for compensating people injured by medicines or doctors is in critical condition. Attempts to tinker with it are doomed to fail for the same reason that healthcare itself resists reform. As long as we frame the healthcare liability problem as a zero-sum competition with a winner for every loser, we will stay paralyzed. Every initiative offered by one side will be automatically resisted by the other. We can argue and sue each other forever, but have we lost sight of the injured patients for whom the system is supposed to bring relief?

We need transformative healthcare liability system reform—not so much tort reform as tort replacement.

Instead of arguing about the existing system, we can get new traction on a solution by considering specialized medical courts as a superior way to deliver the benefits that the healthcare liability system is supposed to, but rarely, provides. There is nothing radical about this model. We already have separate courts to deal with disputes involving workers' compensation, vaccine injuries, patents, and tax liability. If precedent is a guide, the main advantages of specialized medical courts will be expertise, speed, and lower costs. The courts could help determine when care has been substandard and when injury has actually resulted.

The health courts should be nationwide to minimize location-based variability. Funded by fees paid by healthcare providers, the courts would feature a decentralized administrative structure coupled with strong performance incentives and accountability measures. The savings generated by these courts would be available for future healthcare.

As long as we have an adversarial system—two sides, horns locked—we will succeed only at confusing the issues, delaying compensation to the injured, and perpetuating preventable medical error. Trial lawyers retain their "right to sue" when something goes wrong. But that right will be balanced against the rights of healthcare professionals to a system of justice that is more focused on compensating patients than fixing blame.

Patients who have been injured by medical error deserve compensation. I believe that doctors who make mistakes should be held accountable. But there has to be a better way than a system that sweeps up doctors who do no wrong, is almost random in its outcomes, takes years for any resolution, and usually provides injured parties with less than 40 percent of any settlement. This is not an efficient way to either improve quality or compensate injury. Specialized medical courts represent a better way.

The Power of Apology

A related action is to disengage apologies from attachment of liability. The point is to create incentives for doctors to accept as much responsibility for the mistakes as they are willing to accept. Under this doctrine, the relationships between patients and doctors—imperfect human beings doing their best under often difficult circumstances—can operate on a more human level. When a patient is injured, doctors can offer an apology, admit fault, and express regret and sympathy without fearing that the statement will later be used against them in court. The most progressive lawyers recognize that doctors might be overestimating the costs of apologies and underestimating their benefits.[4]

The reality is that healthcare professionals are human and humans make mistakes. Most patients understand this. The rage that arises out of the injury and fuels so much of the animosity is almost always drained away by a sincere "I'm sorry." The refusal to acknowledge a mistake only reinforces a patient's decision to seek a legal remedy. And the failure to accept responsibility might make some patients believe they are *justified* in filing a malpractice claim.

The recent tendency favoring "no fault" litigation is reflected by emerging judicial guidelines that generally prevent expressions of sympathy from being used as evidence of fault after an accident. Three states—California, Texas, and Massachusetts—have passed what are known as "benevolent gestures" or "expressions of sympathy" statutes. These are laws that are intended to make it easier to apologize without liability attaching itself to the statement. What these laws encourage are expressions of sympathy from doctors in the aftermath of an accident or injury without the remarks being used against the doctors in court.

I call on the governors of the states to propose legislation that prevents trial lawyers from using apologies against the doctors who issue them. And I call on health professionals at all levels to issue apologies and statements of regret when a patient has been injured.

Four: Reform Direct-to-Consumer Advertising

DTC advertising can be a powerful public good—making people familiar with various therapies and promoting the primacy of the doctor-patient relationship. Good DTC communication should encourage people to talk with their physicians about their medical conditions. DTC advertising should help demystify sensitive medical problems and encourage people to seek treatment even for conditions stigmatized by society. For all these reasons, I prefer to describe our efforts as DTC education.

However, pharmaceutical companies need to deal with the current public perceptions about this kind of outreach to the patient. DTC advertising can sometimes send the wrong message about the nature of medical treatment. It's time for reform, and I see four areas where immediate changes can be made by all of us doing such outreach.

First is content. All DTC education should be accurate, understandable, and motivating. My commitment as the head of Pfizer is to improve communications about risk. We will work harder to ensure that people understand that no medicine is 100-percent risk-free for every patient. To do that, we at Pfizer are already reaching out to patient and consumer groups to see how we can communicate risk information in ways that consumers more readily understand. We're not alone in this. Johnson & Johnson has already unveiled a series of TV ads that talk about risk in a different way, and I applaud their efforts.

In Pfizer's drive to make DTC education even better, our ads will let patients know when alternative therapies are available, including therapies that do not require a medicine, such as diet and exercise. We will also do more to strengthen the relationship between doctor and patient, emphasizing that doctors are the first and best source for help in making the right therapeutic decisions.

Second is marketing public health. Companies like Pfizer know a great deal about informing and motivating people on health issues. We should use these skills to promote the routes to public health, such as prevention and wellness, compliance with treatment regimens, and disease awareness. All the market research we have done, both in the United States and in Europe, indicates a "pent-up demand" by people for more open channels of communication on all dimensions of health. Companies like Pfizer can help meet this demand. I have already asked Pfizer's marketing professionals for a plan that would focus on several important public health issues and promote them with the same approaches and resources we deploy for marketing a branded pharmaceutical.

Promoting access to medicines is the third area. In the United States, nearly all the major pharmaceutical companies have patient assistance programs to help people in need get the medicines they need. Our industry should do a better job in communicating about these programs and encouraging people to enroll in them. In the United States, a number of pharmaceutical companies have formed the Partnership for Prescription Assistance, which brings together an array of access programs under one brand. I am also committed to more focused communication about Pfizer's many access programs in America, now offered under the umbrella, "Helpful Answers." As this book went to press, Pfizer was mailing out more than three million booklets to our stakeholders promoting these two user-friendly access programs.

I'm committed to including information about "Helpful Answers" in all our print ads and websites. And again, I've asked our marketing professionals to develop plans for a national campaign to increase awareness of, and enrollment in, "Helpful Answers." (I invite readers in America who may need assistance with their Pfizer medicines to phone "Helpful Answers," toll-free, at 866-776-3700.)

The fourth step is external oversight. DTC education must meet high standards of accountability. It makes no sense for us to develop an ad that we think meets these standards, and then be told later that it doesn't. We're ready to find a better way, including working with the FDA to get their views on an advertisement before it is run. We will do whatever we can to support the FDA's role in ensuring that patients benefit from thoughtful and appropriate healthcare messages.

Pfizer will support changes in these four areas. But if we act alone, it won't be enough. I call on other leaders in this industry to join this commitment to reform and ensure that DTC prescription drug education serves patients even better. The need for change is urgent. We can do more with this important communications tool to help save lives, give people more power over their health, and provide more value for every dollar spent in the pursuit of wellness.

Five: Build a Level Playing Field for Health Savings Accounts

Health Savings Accounts (HSAs) pair a high-deductible catastrophic health plan with an individually controlled tax-deductible savings plan. The first plan insures people in the case of a catastrophic medical event. The second plan lets people fund routine medical and preventive care, while letting them save funds for future medical costs and build up a nest egg for retirement.

In order for HSAs to work, they need equal tax treatment. Currently, employees at large organizations have a preferential rate for all health insurance. I call on Congress to enact legislation that puts small businesses and self-employed people on an equal footing. Everyone would then have access to managed care discounts. It would be the best of all worlds: privately delivered insurance that promotes individual responsibility and spurs competition.

To extend the benefits of HSAs to low-income families, I believe the government should provide a direct $1000 contribution to their HSA, along with a refundable $2000 tax credit to help purchase a policy to cover major medical expenses.

Here's an inequity I would like to see ended. As an employee of a large company, part of my health insurance costs are paid for by my employer, and those costs in turn are subsidized by taxpayers in general, many of whom can't even afford health insurance for themselves. But if you are not part of a large corporation that provides healthcare benefits, or self-employed, you don't get that tax benefit. That's not right. I call on Congress to treat all health insurance payments, regardless of who pays them, as tax-deductible. Subsidizing the people with the best jobs does not make sense.

We can't take away the tax benefit from those who already have it. But I do think we can find a way to provide the same or similar tax benefit to those who pay for their own health insurance. HSAs offer a good platform for people to spend pretax dollars for their healthcare.

I believe there is merit in the idea of making health insurance mandatory, much as the way we mandate car insurance. Doing so would "capture" the healthy uninsured, whose absence from the pool makes insurance costlier for the rest of us. This plan could work only if associated with a guaranteed-issue or a high-risk pool, as well as a subsidy for people who couldn't afford it.

In other words, we should have a social contract where everybody buys insurance. It can be a "hard mandate," parallel to the system that requires car liability insurance of all car drivers. Or it can be a "soft mandate" that invokes a number of rewards. For example, people who choose to purchase health insurance might get a tax credit to cover most or all of their health-insurance premiums. But those who choose not to purchase insurance would incur a tax penalty in the form of losing their standard deduction. Under some proposals, the money raised by such penalties would be earmarked to subsidize coverage for those who wanted health insurance but couldn't afford it.

Six: Use Trade Agreements to End Free-Riding

Sometimes I think we should give countries that free-ride on the United States so they can enjoy new drugs at lower prices a taste of their own medicine, if you'll forgive the pun. Here's what I mean. Even though the United States and Australia completed negotiations on a landmark trade agreement that won broad bipartisan support in Congress, a dispute over drugs threatened to derail the agreement. In Australia, there was a loud outcry that the free trade pact could undermine the popular government program that makes prescription drugs available to all citizens at low prices. In other words, Australia wants free trade in everything else but clings to price controls for drugs under Australia's national health insurance program

Now, Australia makes some fine wines. I like their wine and my cellar has a lot of excellent Australian vintages. But I don't like paying the prices of Australian wine. What if we tell Australia, "Okay, we'll have free trade in wine, but we won't pay more than $5 per bottle"? That's exactly what's happening in pharmaceuticals. Australia tells us that we'll have free trade in prescription medicines, but they won't pay more than 50 percent of the U.S. price. The result is that prices for new drugs in Australia are among the lowest in the developed world.

Where is the fairness in this? You can't have free trade when one party artificially reduces the prices of the second. That's beggar-your-neighbor trade policy of the worst kind. If we're going to import foreign goods and allow Australian, Canadian, and European producers to sell in the free markets of the United States, we should be able to sell our products in Australia, Canada, and Europe free of artificial price controls. I call on the governments of all countries to end their beggar-your-neighbor policies. The result will be a more equitable sharing of the costs of research and development.

Let's put an end to other countries free-riding on the United States. If the developed nations of the world paid their fair share of the R&D costs required to develop new medicines, then the pharmaceutical industry could afford to provide medicines to the developing world at very low prices or, as is Pfizer's policy, free of charge. There is no market for some of our products in many parts of the developing world. The reality is we are not going to sell any product at any price. But our marginal costs are so low that if we can spread the cost of development out a little broader, we can absorb the cost of providing products free of charge in these areas. We want to do this, but we can't do it alone.

Let's take the case of UK 427-857, our new CCR5-blocker AIDS medicine. If we have to earn a return on that investment only in the United States, then it becomes more difficult to provide it at low cost or free to the people of the developing nations of the world who so desperately need it.

I'd like to explore this point of concern in our negotiations with developed countries if this new medicine becomes available. They will want this new CCR5 medicine, but if precedent holds, by holding down the price they are willing to pay for the new drug, the burden will be shifted to patients in the United States—who have to pay the full amount—and to Pfizer—which then finds it more difficult to provide this lifesaving medicine at affordable prices to those who cannot afford to pay any price at all.

Seven: Maintain Incentives for Innovation

Success in the pharmaceutical sector depends on the political will of governments to provide the right mix of incentives for what is inherently a high-risk, high-reward business. Let me mention just two incentives that I believe will contribute to the development of more biomedical innovation and intellectual property for the benefit of the world.

First, I call for patent regulations to start the clock on the day pharmaceutical products are introduced to the market.[5] This is the standard that is true of almost every other manufactured product.

We can thank the Founding Fathers for a patent system that has catalyzed the most innovative society in history. For the most part, the patent system works pretty well. If you invent a device that automatically turns on the windshield wipers on your car when it starts to rain, society sends a message through the patent system that that innovation is desirable. The message is, "That's a good invention. You should be rewarded for that, and your reward is that you alone will have 20 years to profit from your invention. The clock starts ticking when the patent is registered. Good luck."

But pharmaceutical companies rarely have anywhere close to 20 years to benefit from their discovery of a new drug. If you discover a cure for cancer, society says, "That's a good discovery. You should be rewarded for that, and your reward is that when the medicine is demonstrated to be safe and effective you will have a chance to profit from your discovery. The clock starts ticking when the patent is registered. Good luck."

The complication is that the process of making a medicine ready for market generally takes 10-15 years. Stated another way, from the time it starts to sell a medicine, the drug company that developed it might have 10 years or less before the patent expires. As a result, the company has a much shorter period in which it attempts to profit from its work. This is a disincentive to create new drugs, and because companies have to generate revenues over a shorter period of time, it increases the prices of the medicines that are created.

Second, I call for the creation of incentives to promote vaccine R&D. Such incentives would not only help encourage the development of vaccines in general, but represent the best strategy for targeting the diseases affecting developing nations.

Vaccine R&D for diseases that primarily affect developing countries is inadequate. Market conditions are unlikely to reverse the dynamics that keep firms from spending the millions of dollars necessary to develop products to fight these diseases. I call on the United States to create, join, and encourage the creation of advance markets for vaccines for HIV, malaria, and other diseases. Purchase commitments like that announced by Gordon Brown, Britain's Chancellor of the Exchequer, provide the pull mechanism required to spur companies to take on the risk of developing vaccines, especially for the diseases devastating the people of developing nations. "These programs reward success without micromanaging the research process and may mark the start of a trend that could save tens of millions of lives—particularly if private donors take the cue," write Michael Kremer and Rachel Glennerster, authors of *Strong Medicine: Creating Incentives for Pharmaceutical Research on Neglected Diseases.*[6]

Here's how a typical plan might work. The sponsors pledge $3 billion to buy a malaria vaccine at $15 per person for the first 200 million people immunized. The result is a pot that compares in size to what a company could expect in the wake of a successful drug launch. "If purchase commitments fail to induce the development of new vaccines, no money will be spent. But if they succeed, millions of lives will be saved each year," Kremer and Glennerster suggest.[7]

A more direct action would be for a government or consortium of governments to offer a transferable, five-year extension to any pharmaceutical patent for the development of a successful vaccine. Such a "wild card" prize might be enough to spur an organization to take the risk of turning medical research into a viable vaccine product. History tells us this approach can work.[8]

Eight: Demand Electronic Medical Records

I call for action to make electronic medical records universally available for Americans in the next 10 years. Information technology is bringing down the curtain on those who believe that denying patients access to information is a way to control costs. That approach was never right, and is useless in a wired world. To help conquer the cost of disease, healthcare systems must give people access to clear and timely information. They must help free medical professionals from excessive bureaucracy and help them avoid mistakes in serving patients.

Electronic medical records go a long way towards meeting these goals. Every healthcare payer, every taxpayer, should be demanding them today. Managing medical records electronically is less expensive and saves lives. But to *start* millions of people on paper medical records instead of electronic ones in this day and age is stunningly shortsighted. Unfortunately, with the Welcome to Medicare physical, that is what we are doing. I call on the government to document the Welcome to Medicare physical as an electronic medical record. Every 65-year-old who wants to enroll in Medicare needs to take this physical exam. The Welcome to Medicare visit is a moment in time, but preventive care is a continuum. With seniors living 25 to 35 years after this physical, does anyone really think it's cheaper to maintain these records on paper forms that have to be copied and mailed?

The Welcome to Medicare visit is a unique opportunity to deliver prevention services. The goal is to assist seniors to focus on the health behaviors that prevent disease and to identify the screening tests and immunizations for which they are due. In the Welcome to Medicare visit, physicians should be asking about tobacco use, when patients were last screened for breast cancer or immunized against influenza, the details of their physical activity, and diet. If the visit were to generate an electronic record, the physician could do a much better job of recommending and delivering preventive services that would have a profound impact on both the senior and the healthcare system on which the senior will rely.

Collecting this data electronically not only saves money, but it also benefits patients on an individual level by offering them customized health services. It creates opportunities to recruit private partners to deliver innovative prevention services. The giant consumer market created by the millions of seniors who are entitled to the Welcome to Medicare visit each year will entice commercial entities and partners to offer exciting new services at attractive prices.

The full benefits of the Welcome to Medicare visit cannot be realized without leveraging the delivery of preventive services through a systems solution. Reminder systems, both those designed for doctors and reminders sent to patients, can be an important reinforcement tool that promotes preventive services. Electronic medical records facilitate such reminders and provide useful tools for tracking adherence to a health maintenance plan. Electronic medical records give computer-literate patients greater control over their health. Just one example of how such a system can be used: seniors could print summaries of their records to bring to their appointments. The system would later send patients e-mails to remind them to obtain follow-up screening tests, fill a prescription, or contact them when new supplies of flu vaccine become available.

Nine: Report on Corporate Citizenship

Corporate citizenship at Pfizer means considering our plans and actions against one profound question: What will our children think? At its core, corporate citizenship means being a responsible business in the short and long term for shareholders at large. To communicate that, we must report to the world on our activities as corporate citizens as frequently and as forthrightly as we report on our financial performance.

I call on all public companies to issue reports on the corporate citizenship activities of their organizations. Such reports should join financial reports as a way for people to gauge the overall performance of publicly-held companies.

Some people call it corporate social responsibility. To me, the term "corporate citizenship" best describes the concept that all parts of society have a role, responsibility, and opportunity to participate in creating and sustaining a healthy society. For companies, it means we are part of the solution at every level of engagement, from patients to employees to communities. I am committing Pfizer to good corporate citizenship on five levels:

1. Advancing good health
2. Exchanging issues and ideas
3. Protecting the environment
4. Conducting business responsibly
5. Empowering employees

Every quarter, Pfizer issues a Performance Report detailing our activities in three areas: financial, corporate citizenship, and access to medicine. In my view, all three are important measures of our performance.

Delivering on the promise of healthcare described in this book is unthinkable in the absence of a robust commitment to corporate citizenship in every one of these areas. For example, we advance good health by reaching out to patients, physicians, government officials, caregivers, and critics. We want to hear their concerns and needs, and to inform them of the latest information and practices around the themes described in this book. The *Florida: A Healthy State* program is an example of a public-private partnership that I believe represents a more responsible model for caring for people in a patient-centered, community-based healing network. We also advance good health by making medicines accessible (for example, our Helpful Answers program) or partnering with experts in different fields to deliver the benefits of Pfizer research to developing nations (the Infectious Disease Institute or the International Trachoma Initiative).

I don't have the space here to describe all our efforts in this area, but readers can find more details at www.pfizer.com/corporatecitizenship.

I invite you to review our programs and contact me with your questions and suggestions.

Ten: Initiate a Global Health Corps

The Peace Corps offers us a valuable model of activism and building infrastructure. I call for the creation of a Global Health Corps, an international program under which trained healthcare professionals from the developed world would put their talents to work in medically underserved areas in developing nations. I know from my own son and his medical school classmates that young doctors want to do what they can to alleviate suffering. Well-trained healthcare professionals are eager to dedicate themselves to something like a Global Health Corps. This is a proposal I actually made to President George W. Bush when he asked me for my ideas about healthcare. I suggested that we make the program available to physicians, nurses, epidemiologists, medical technicians, scientists, business experts, anybody with the skills and energy to spend six months to a year helping build worldwide infrastructure for health.

This call to action is the basis for the Pfizer Global Health Fellows program. As this book went to press, the third class of Global Health Fellows began their tours. This class paired 21 Pfizer employees from

North America and Europe with nongovernmental organizations (NGOs) and a U.S. government initiative to help fight diseases including HIV/AIDS, trachoma, tuberculosis, and malaria in Africa and Asia.

The Fellows utilize their skills in science and technology to train researchers and healthcare providers, develop and implement communications programs, and upgrade facilities and technological resources.

Global Health Fellows are selected through a competitive process, in part for their desire to make a difference in the world, their strengths in teaching and training, and their enthusiasm to see their work carried on by local teams. Pfizer foots the bill for the trip and continues to pay the volunteers their full salary for the duration of their service.

Pfizer colleagues are now working with NGOs in Africa and Latin America. We believe this is a good investment on a number of levels. Our Fellows have the skills and experience to make a real difference for people in the world. They come back with a renewed sense of purpose, a dedication to teamwork, and firsthand experience with problems that exist and solutions that actually work. Pfizer is a stronger company for having employees with such experience.

CHAPTER 14

THE DEADLINE FOR COMPLAINTS WAS YESTERDAY

The core message of this book is that the solution to the crisis in healthcare is not rationing or price controls but investment in health.

Prevention is more than good intentions or even applied resources. In order for prevention to truly work, we need cultural change at every level. Car crashes associated with people driving under the influence of alcohol continue to be a preventable killer of tens of thousands of Americans a year. We can talk about all kinds of prevention—improving driver education, increasing penalties—but true change is not possible until people are emotionally engaged with the problem in an entirely new way. To make healthcare prevention truly a part of people's lives, I believe we will need to make the appeal on both intellectual and emotional levels.

Prevention is critical because healthcare is always going to consume *more* of our income. We will want to spend more on healthcare five years from now than we do now. How can it be otherwise? Our populations are aging, and advances in medical care to extend and promote the quality of life are expensive. I share with you a vision of people at every age level secure in their healthcare systems. The question is, "What are the institutions that can take us there?"

The chronic diseases that claim lives and contribute mightily to the rising costs of healthcare around the world are caused largely by preventable or manageable personal behaviors. Fully 35 percent of deaths in America are caused by three behaviors: tobacco use, poor diet, and physical inactivity.

Habits can be broken. Preventive services—in which doctors help patients change these behaviors, provide vaccines to prevent infectious diseases, and use screening tests to catch diseases in their early stages— deserve greater attention from policymakers. Our healthcare system expends most of its resources on interventions and procedures—reacting to existing disease. But investing in prevention could be much more effective. Treatments for cardiovascular disease can save 4000-10,000 lives per year. But helping Americans to stop smoking would save more than 400,000.

Prevention makes sense not only for the fundamental reason that it improves health, but also for economic reasons. The cost of treating the complications of diseases is enormous. When it comes to health, we know that it is simply good business to pay for prevention rather than procedures. It's a morally bankrupt system that pats itself on the back for patching up those it allows to fall through the social safety net. Arkansas Governor Mike Huckabee said it best: "Our health care system should build a fence at the top of the cliff so we can stop sending ambulances to the bottom."[1]

Assets Our Children Can Live With

Life and health are our ultimate assets. Everything else flows from these values. Every one of the actions proposed in this book are driven by my conviction that the healthcare systems of the world, as dysfunctional and wasteful as they are, represent enormous opportunity. I know it's tempting to define the healthcare systems of the world by what they are not, by what they lack, and how they fall short. But I say institutions are marginalized when they define themselves by emptiness.

Success flows from a focus on assets, not deficits. We have our best shot of attaining twenty-first century healthcare systems not by focusing on the holes, deficiencies, and limitations, but by seizing on healthcare as a collective of strengths and accomplishments. This is the attitude that I believe will give us a healthcare system our children can live with.

This book comes out of my conviction that health is an asset and that sound investments in assets are desirable. We must abandon the historical strategy of treating healthcare as a cost to be avoided. We cannot cost-shift our way to health. I have argued that the solution to the healthcare spending crisis will not come from shrinking the bottom line through failed strategies such as rationing and price controls. Nor do we need significantly more money than we are already spending. The solution to the crisis will come from expanding the top line by investing in the health and wellness of people.

We have seen that sickness drains societies of wealth. The converse is demonstrably true, as well. A system focused on prevention, education, and early intervention, backed up by the best-trained physicians and the latest therapies and medications, allows its citizens to live longer, work smarter, and contribute more. Societies that put the individual in the center of healthcare, leaving no one out, encourage the development of healthy people secure in the face of health challenges. They have the confidence to marry, bring children into the world, and start businesses. Health creates the fabric of civil societies.

The fight against poverty starts with health. Also critical to the mix are representative governments, absence of corruption, free trade, free markets, education, and respect for the rule of law. Put all of these attributes together and you have my prescription for eradicating poverty from the planet.

Transforming Healthcare

I opened this book with an anecdote about Gandhi, so perhaps it is fitting that I close with another nod to the Mahatma. In the wake of his triumph over the liberation of India after 300 years of British colonialism, Gandhi provided the formula for those who desire change: *"First they ignore you. Then they laugh at you. Then they fight you. Then you win."*

These words provide hope to those committed to a goal nearly as daunting—the liberation of our healthcare systems from more than a century of zero-sum elitism, waste, and failed policies.

We have an opportunity in the next decade to create a healthcare system worthy of a society that values health, innovation, inclusiveness, and personal autonomy. My hope is that transformation of the current model along the lines described in this book will put individuals in the center, empowered by the knowledge to take control of their health and, when necessary, their own healthcare.

Transforming healthcare is a massive task, and systematic transformation is what it will take. The current model puts emphasis on everything but health. It is misfocused in defining sickness as the center of the system and acute interventions as its primary interest. With its lack of competition, accountability, and transparency, it distributes power to everyone but the individual patient.

Reforming the system through incremental steps is akin to making a skyscraper taller by cannibalizing construction materials from the lower floors. The very principle of a third-party payer system is subversive to sound healthcare because restraint flies out the window when you have a triangular-payment model where a service is delivered by one party, consumed by a second, and paid for by a third. All that cost-shifting does is breed conflict.

Closing the Gap

There is an enormous gap between the healthcare we know our society is capable of attaining and the healthcare we have presently. For those of us with health insurance, the problem is cost, which keeps going up at double-digit levels. For those without health insurance, the problem is access, which keeps going down as services are rationed. For everyone, regardless of coverage, the problem is the apprehension that we have been poor stewards of the healthcare system. Evaluated against my father's adage that we show our gratitude by returning something we've borrowed in better condition than when we received it, our performance has not been promising. Unless we act now, we must prepare ourselves for the real possibility that the healthcare system our children inherit will not be as good as the one that was left to us.

Advocates of healthcare transformation can take heart from the experience of welfare reform. The American welfare system was long thought to be incapable of reform. This statement was accurate: welfare couldn't be reformed; it had to be deconstructed and rebuilt in a new image. For over 25 years, we were told to be realistic and settle for incremental adjustments to an inherently bad system.

Eventually the moral and financial bankruptcy of the existing system could not be ignored. More and more voices—including those of Welfare recipients themselves—demanded change. In 1996, a cycle of dependency that made generations of families passive recipients of public aid was gradually changed by the requirement that recipients get a job or go to school. Support services were put in place to ease the transition from dependency to opportunity. Though opponents trotted out frightening scenarios of starving children, the transformation is achieving the desired benefits. The promised calamities have yet to materialize.

So it will be for healthcare transformation. The forces of obstructionism will put up a fight, but they will lose. It took 25 years before the problems with welfare reached the tipping point. Transforming healthcare will happen much faster. Everyone has a stake in their health and in the health of their loved ones. The people who stand to gain the most from the transformation have voices, and they will be heard.

As with the welfare system, it's time to deconstruct healthcare. The greatest opportunities in healthcare occur before people get sick. Personal experience and scientific studies demonstrate that health policies encouraging prevention, early intervention, nutrition, and exercise are effective in saving lives and money. A transformed approach starts with an individual-centered program of health management. It requires individuals to have real ownership in the resources of healthcare. It demands a tight link between an individual's economic self-interest and personal health. The current model, which is payer-centered and focused on acute care, cannot deliver these opportunities.

No individual can describe the entire challenge nor provide all the solutions. We each have a piece of the puzzle, a fragment of the mosaic. I have an abiding confidence that the solutions to our healthcare problems are within reach. I am ready to participate in any forum that brings together people committed to finding new solutions for our common challenges. I'm grateful for the optimism infused in me by my children and the resolve instilled in me by my parents.

No one pretends that victory will be easy. Making these transformations will require massive shifts in resources and priorities. Although the benefits to society will be substantial, powerful constituencies will lose power and privilege. The people reading this book will be asked to share the burden of building a more equitable healthcare infrastructure. We mustn't look away from the certainty that the healthcare systems of the world can be transformed without significant cost to ourselves.

We avoid this cost only at the risk of forsaking a sacred promise to those who depend on us. Any attempt to defer these costs distances us from life itself. In the depths of the sacrifice is the strength we need to live fully and build a better world and better health for our children. Embracing this opportunity is not for the faint of heart, but then again, neither is life.

EPILOGUE

Water. Life is impossible without it. Sometimes life is destroyed by it. As a sailor, I know. Water will break your heart.

Like the rest of the world, I heard the first news reports of the tsunami early on the day after Christmas. The first accounts described widespread destruction along the beachfront communities and islands of the Indian Ocean. Initial casualties were estimated in the tens of thousands. My heart sank, not only because I anticipated that the death toll would be far higher, but also because I feared this disaster would touch Pfizer colleagues and their families directly. We have thousands of colleagues in the region and the beaches of Thailand are vacation destinations very popular with our colleagues in Europe.

The Tsunami of 2004 has entered the record books as one of the greatest destructive natural disasters of the past 500 years. Certainly, it is the one that's been most documented, from the agonizing amateur videos showing the waves coming ashore to the massive global media coverage of the recovery and relief efforts. The final death toll will never be known. As this book went to press, bodies were still being recovered. The number of people killed or missing and presumed dead may exceed 300,000. Among these people were 4 Pfizer colleagues and 19 members of their families.

The natural forces of the world are sometimes destructive. But human compassion and the willingness to help are also natural forces. In the aftermath of the tsunami that devastated the shores of the Indian

Ocean in December 2004, the response of the world was overwhelming. When the world's attention is focused on a humanitarian challenge, we can be heartened by what people of good will can accomplish. In the end we are measured not by the magnitude of the disaster, but by our response.

Within hours of the news reports, Pfizer colleagues stepped up to the humanitarian challenges. Remarkably, some of our colleagues in Asia formed their own search parties to scour beaches and search open-air hospitals and makeshift morgues for missing colleagues and their families. Some of these Pfizer colleagues put their own lives at risk to do this. I told these colleagues, and the 115,000 others that make up Pfizer's world, that sometimes our greatest assets cannot be measured by financial statements or balance sheets. At a time when companies are often portrayed as heartless, the individual heroism of these colleagues and so many others will be one of my most cherished memories as a corporate leader.

Pfizer itself went on to donate about $60 million—$10 million in cash and more than $50 million in medicines and other supplies—to relief efforts. My colleagues around the world dug into their own pockets for additional donations while other Pfizer colleagues went to the affected areas to take on the hard work of reconstruction. Four weeks after the disaster, I personally visited the area. Another book will be required to describe what I saw.

The resources of the world are continuing to flow to the devastated regions. The tsunami underscored for me the fragility and preciousness of life. It also reinforced the tremendous capacity for people to respond when life is threatened.

One of the hardest aspects of life for those affected by natural disasters is the sense of loss of control. Within minutes, one's family might be wiped out, a home destroyed, all possessions lost. On December 26, 2004, millions of people were thrust into a situation where they owned nothing but their lives. A precious gift preserved, to be sure, but perhaps the most disorienting experience one could ever envision. We may not have control over all dimensions of our lives, but we like to think we have some say in our destiny. Millions of people lost all of this on Tsunami Day, 2004.

As this book goes to press, ownership is a concept much in the news. The central question of the day is how much personal responsibility should individuals take over their social security, pensions, retirement accounts, and, health savings accounts. I want to extend that dialogue to another aspect of ownership.

I believe that every person should accept ownership of their health. This includes working for public health as well as individual health, for one is quite impossible without the other. Taking ownership of one's health is not easy. It can be difficult work, but unlike paying for surgery or medicines, it doesn't have to cost you a penny.

I envision a healthcare system that engages people before they become sick. Prevention, early intervention, education—the central themes of this book—represent a contract to make such a healthcare system possible.

There are no guarantees, of course. Everyone could lose weight, eat oat bran noon and night, and walk everywhere, and some people would still have heart attacks. But, on average, prevention represents the safest bet any of us can make. I support the widespread use of the best medicine of all: prevention. Prevention is nothing less than a contract with long-term health. If you exercise an hour a day, eat right, and don't smoke, you'll probably live longer and better and need fewer procedures and drugs in the long run. This is the basis of a healthcare system we can all support, and will support all of us when we truly need help.

I began writing this book as a newly minted grandfather with a sense that we need to do more to create a world of health for our grandchildren. Sarah has already celebrated her first birthday. Soon she will be talking and asking questions. I hope my answers will satisfy her.

Little in this life is free. A glance from a granddaughter is one of them. Let us put our hearts and minds together to see what future we can build for our grandchildren. She and millions of other small children are counting on us. We must not let them down.

ENDNOTES

Chapter 2

1 The challenge of defining health is similar to what the economist John Kenneth Galbraith faced in 1958 when he sought to examine poverty and its causes. Poverty, then as now, was unremarkable, the unrelenting experience of millions of human beings. Galbraith's insight was to study the conditions that caused the *absence* of poverty. Thus was born *The Affluent Society*, a book that inspired policymakers to think differently about poverty and affluence, resulting in less of the former and more of the latter. So it is with healthcare. For too long, the focus has been on sickness, disease, and chronic illness. These are conditions that, like poverty, are all too real. Let's focus our energies on the *absence* of illness; in other words, health.

2 *Stedman's Medical Dictionary*. Baltimore: William-Wilkins, 1995.

3 In Mitch Albom's best-selling book *Tuesdays with Morrie*, we are privileged to meet Morris Schwartz, who is dying of Amyotrophic Lateral Sclerosis or ALS—also known as Lou Gehrig's disease. Morrie eventually succumbs to a devastating disease that we still cannot cure, although we keep trying. His final months are no one's ideal of health. Yet his attitude of well-being in the face of ALS inspires us to live to the limits of what is possible. Clearly, health is more than just a matter of physiology or cell biology—and it means something broader than absence of infirmity.

Chapter 3

1 Jones, Harvey. "Take Sting out of Health Cover: Can new range of policies offer protection without breaking the bank?" *London Daily Express*, October 30, 2004, p. 44-45.

2 Goetzel, Ron Z., Long, Stacey R., et al. "Health, Absence, Disability, and Presenteeism Cost Estimates of Certain Physical and Mental Health Conditions Affecting US Employers," *Journal of Occupational and Environmental Medicine*, April 2004.

3 Cubbin, James C. Testimony before the Federal Trade Commission, November 7, 1995.

Chapter 4

1 Today, America's uninsured do not have to pay full retail price for their Pfizer medicines. They can go to almost any retail pharmacy in the country and save money immediately. Readers can find more information about Pfizer Helpful Answers at www.pfizer.com or by calling toll free, 1-866-776-3700.

2 HelpingPatients helps direct patients to the patient assistance program that will best serve them. HelpingPatients also contains a database of all the member companies that conduct these programs and the medicines that are covered. The service also describes how to request assistance. Readers can get more information about HelpingPatients by pointing their browsers to www.helpingpatients.org.

3 The wholesale price is the price drug makers charge large pharmacies and distributors. Drug companies have no control over retail prices.

4 Espicom Business Intelligence, *World Pharmaceutical Markets*, 2003, p. 108. Data refers to PhRMA manufacturer's prices for prescription drug sales only, not OTC or generics. Similar statis-

tics aggregating brand-name, OTC and generic medicines are published by the Centers for Medicare & Medicaid Services, Office of the Actuary, National Health Statistics Group, *National Health Accounts, State Health Expenditures.* Health, United States, 2004 and Health, United States, 1980.

5   Colvin, Geoffrey. "We Hate Big Pharma—but We Sure Love Drugs." *Fortune*, December 27, 2004, p. 56.

6   Dietz, Elizabeth. "Trends in employer-provided prescription-drug coverage," *Monthly Labor Review*, August 2004, p. 81. The percentage of workers covered by indemnity plans with a $10 or greater copayment for brand-name prescription drugs increased from 19 percent in 1993 to 79 percent in 2000, while the percentage covered by prepaid plans increased from 10 percent in 1993 to 78 percent in 2000. See also www.bls.gov/opub/ted/2004/oct/wk1/art01.htm

7   Kaiser Family Foundation Report, Trends and Indicators in the Changing Health Care Marketplace, 2004. See especially Exhibit 1.21: Profitability Among Pharmaceutical Manufacturers Compared to Other Industries, 1995-2003. For every year from 1995 through 2002, the pharmaceutical industry was the most profitable industry in the United States, although its profitability declined somewhat in 2002. In 2003, drug companies ranked as the third most profitable industry (14.3 percent). Drug companies were more than three times as profitable as the median for all *Fortune* 500 companies in 2003 (14.3 percent compared to 4.6 percent). http://www.kff.org/insurance/7031/ti2004-1-21.cfm

8   *Fortune* magazine, Global 500, 1975 data. www.fortune.com

9   Ibid.

10 Consolidation removed some companies from the list (Sandoz and Ciba-Geigy merged to create Novartis; Warner-Lambert was acquired by Pfizer; American Home Products by Wyeth). Others were replaced by more innovative American companies. In 1975, 20 percent of the top 10 pharmaceutical companies were based in America; by 2004, American firms represented 50 percent.

Chapter 5

1 Hensley, Scott. "As Drug-Sales Teams Multiply, Doctors Start to Tune Them Out." *The Wall Street Journal*, June 13, 2003.
2 National Institute for Health Care Management (NIHCM). (2001) Prescription drug spending in 2001: The upward trend continues.
3 Gladwell, Malcolm. "High Prices: How to Think About Prescription Drugs," *The New Yorker*, October 25, 2004, pp. 86-90.

Chapter 6

1 Friedman, Milton, *et al*. "Economists Warn of Dangers of Drug Importation, Price Controls." *Health Care News*, February 1, 2004.
2 "Researchers are Testing 79 Medicines and Vaccines for HIV and Opportunistic Infections." Medicines in Development for HIV/AIDs: 2004 Survey. Pharmaceutical Research and Manufacturers of America. Available at http://www.phrma.org/newmedicines/resources/2004-11-30.146.pdf

Chapter 7

1 I acknowledge Scott Adams, the author of the Dilbert comic strip, for this phrasing of an ancient joke. The strip appeared December 10, 2004.
2 Porter, Michael E., and Teisburg, Elizabeth Olmsted. "Redefining Competition in Health Care." *Harvard Business Review*, June 2004.
3 Ibid.
4 Herzlinger, Regina. *Market Driven Health Care: Who Wins, Who Loses in the Transformation of America's Largest Service Industry*. Cambridge, MA: Perseus Books, p. 166.
5 Herzlinger, Regina, p. 162.
6 Lancaster, John. "Surgeries, Side Trips for 'Medical Tourists': Affordable Care at India's Private Hospitals Draws Growing Number of Foreigners." Washington Post Foreign Service,

Thursday, October 21, 2004; p. A01. Part of the discrepancy in death rates is a function of the relatively healthier patients selected by Escorts.

7   Ibid.

8   Porter, Michael E., and Teisburg, Elizabeth Olmsted. "Redefining Competition in Health Care." *Harvard Business Review*, June 2004. p. 14.

9   Dugger, Celia W. "Lacking Doctors, Africa Is Training Substitutes." *New York Times*, November 23, 2004.

Chapter 8

1   Healthcare insurance is treated differently than other insurance products in the way it is taxed (preferentially) and delivered (through employers). I know that most employers offer their employees life insurance as a matter of course. But the policies tend to be modest and few employees regard this benefit as anything more than marginal to their family's insurance needs.

2   Porter, Michael E., and Teisburg, Elizabeth Olmsted. "Redefining Competition in Health Care." *Harvard Business Review*, June 2004. p. 11.

3   "The Economic Value of Medical Research," Kevin Murphy and Robert Topel, the University of Chicago.

4   Lichtenberg, Frank R. "The benefits to society of new drugs: a survey of the econometric evidence," Proceedings, Federal Reserve Bank of Dallas, September, 2003, pp. 43-59.

5   Steven Covey, the author of *The Seven Habits of Highly Effective People*, has recently suggested the same idea: that a Statue of Responsibility on the West Coast be erected as a companion to the Statue of Liberty on the East Coast. Covey has suggested that Seattle harbor is a suitable site for the Statue of Responsibility. A similar idea was also the unfulfilled dream of the psychotherapist Victor Frankl (1905-1997), author of *Man's Search for Meaning*.

Chapter 9

1   Gingrich, Newt. *Saving Lives & Saving Money: Transforming Health and Healthcare*. Washington, DC: The Alexis de Tocqueville Institution, 2003.

2   Prewo, Wilfried. From *Welfare State to Social State: Empowerment, Individual Responsibility, and Effective Compassion*. Centre for the New Europe, 2004.

3   With the proliferation of healthcare advice, consumers will need to exercise wisdom about the sources to trust. For example, can medicines be "rated" in the same way as DVD players and washing machines? The Consumer's Union, which publishes the respected *Consumer Reports* magazine, purports to be able to do just that. I have my doubts. The goal is to help patients save money by switching to generic drugs or other prescription drugs that *Consumer Reports* says may be just as effective as other medications the patient could be taking and might be less expensive. This is a laudable goal, but it should be done in partnership with patients and doctors. Even though Pfizer came out well in the ratings (the magazine chose Lipitor as the top medication for those who need to lower their cholesterol level by 40 percent), I continue to believe that patients should take medical advice from their doctors, not lists in consumer magazines. My concern is that readers will look at incomplete information and draw inappropriate conclusions about bio-equivalence and efficacy that simply aren't warranted. Fundamentally, I believe such a list undermines the role of the physician in determining best treatment options on a patient-by-patient basis.

4   Remarks by Aetna CEO John Rowe at the Consumer-Directed Healthcare Conference, Washington DC, December 6-8, 2004.

5   PruHealth members earn "vitality" points for pro-health activities: working out at the gym, giving up tobacco use, improving body-fat ratios, lowering cholesterol levels, etc. The more points they accumulate in a year, the cheaper the premiums will be. Theoretically, it is possible for determined

members to accumulate enough points to completely offset
their insurance premiums for that year. For more information,
see htttp://www.pruhealth.co.uk/

6   McGee, Michael. "The Patient-Physician Relationship: Part 1—
Its Role in Society." Available at www.healthpolitics.com/program
transcript.asp?p=prog 25

Chapter 10

1   Rilke, Rainer Maria, "The Man Watching." Rilke (1875-1926)
was an Austro-German lyric poet, author of *Duino Elegies* and
Sonnets to Orpheus.

2   Crawford, Dorothy H. *The Invisible Enemy: A Natural History of
Viruses*. London: Oxford University Press, 2003. There is some
dispute about the accuracy of the quotation attributed to former
Surgeon General Stewart. He is quoted to this effect in the fore-
word by Anthony Epstein but the attribution is not referenced.
See also, Lallanilla, Marc. ABC News original broadcast. "As
New Strains of Bacteria Threaten Public Health, the Government and the Drug Industry Struggle to Keep Up." Nov. 11,
2004. http://abcnews.go.com/Health/story?id=241755&page=1

3   Institute of Medicine and Board on Global Health. *Microbial
Threats to Health: Emergence, Detection, and Response*. Washington, DC: The National Academies Press, 2003.

4   Antibiotic trial without comparator would lower R&D cost, *"The
Pink Sheet."* September 29, 2003.

5   The Infectious Disease Institute in Uganda is a tangible example
of this commitment. The goal is not to do research on new
antimicrobials at the commercial level, but rather to apply what
we have already learned in the prevention and treatment of a
devastating disease.

6   The Vaccine Adverse Event Reporting System (VAERS) is a
national vaccine safety surveillance program cosponsored by
the Food and Drug Administration (FDA) and the Centers for

Disease Control and Prevention (CDC). The purpose of
VAERS is to detect possible signals of adverse events associated
with vaccines. VAERS collects and analyzes information from
reports of adverse events (possible side effects) that occur after
the administration of U.S. licensed vaccines. Health care
providers are required by law to report reactions. For more
information: www.fda.gov/cber/vaers/faq.htm

7 Kremer, Michael, and Glennerster, Rachel. "A Magnet for
Vaccines." *Fortune*, December 27, 2004. p. 52.

8 James, Henry. *The Middle Years*. New York: 1909, p. 105.

Chapter 11

1 Kohn L., Corrigan J., Donaldson M. *To err is human: building a
safer health system*. Washington, DC: Institute of Medicine,
National Academy Press, 1999.

2 Gingrich, Newt, "Post Election Health Care Insights and Implications for the Next Four Years." Remarks at the Consumer-
Directed Healthcare Conference, Washington DC, November
29, 2004. See also Lohr, Steven. "Bush's Next Target:
Malpractice Lawyers." *New York Times*: February 27, 2005.

3 Kohn L., Corrigan J., Donaldson, M. *To err is human: building a
safer health system*. Washington, DC: Institute of Medicine,
National Academy Press, 1999.

4 Safe Practices for Better Healthcare. May 2003. National Quality
Forum. This report details 30 healthcare safe practices that should
be universally utilized in applicable clinical care settings to reduce
the risk of harm to patients. http://www.qualityforum.org/
txsafeexecsumm+order6-8-03PUBLIC.pdf

Chapter 12

1 Singer, Isaac Bashevis, Yiddish-American writer (1904-1991).

2   Calculating the historical exchange rate in Middle Eastern and Asian countries is not easy. Yet tools provided by Professor Wong Ka Fu, of the Department of Economics at the Chinese University of Hong Kong make it easier. See http://intl.econ.cuhk.edu.hk/ exchange_rate_regime/index.php?cid=25

3   Wines, Michael, and LaFraniere, Sharon; "Hut by Hut, AIDS Steals Life in a Southern Africa Town." *New York Times*: November 28, 2004.

4   Acemoglu, Daron and Linn, Joshua. *Quarterly Journal of Economics*, Market Size in Innovation: Theory and Evidence from the Pharmaceutical Industry, April 2004.

5   Friedman, Milton *et al.* "Economists Warn of Dangers of Drug Importation, Price Controls." *Health Care News*, February 1, 2004.

Chapter 13

1   There are many cardiovascular risk formulas and ratios that use your waist measurement, but one of the simplest is also one of the most accurate: Your waist size in inches should not be greater than one-half your height in inches. The greater your abdominal girth relative to your height, the greater your risk of cardiovascular disease.

2   Harris Poll. The Pfizer Journal Survey on Preventative Cardiovascular Health. www.pfizerjournal.com. 2003.

3   Centers for Disease Control. "A Public Health Action Plan to Prevent Heart Disease and Stroke," 2004.

4   Jonathan R. Cohen, a law professor at the University of Florida, estimates that 30 percent of all medical malpractice cases would never require legal intervention if doctors simply apologized for procedures that resulted in injury. Instead, most standard medical malpractice insurance contracts specifically instruct the doctor not to apologize, and more egregiously, to stay completely away from the injured party

once it is clear that the procedure did not result in the intended outcome.

5 This problem has been partly addressed by the Patent Term Restoration Act, in which drug companies get back a portion of the time a drug spends in registration.

6 Kremer, Michael and Glennerster, Rachel. *Strong Medicine : Creating Incentives for Pharmaceutical Research on Neglected Diseases*, Princeton, NJ: Princeton University Press, 2004. p. 52

7 Ibid.

8 Perhaps the most famous pull program in modern history was a cash prize offered by the British government in 1714 to the successful developer of a sturdy sea-going chronometer—a clock sufficiently durable and precise to permit navigators to accurately measure longitude over long voyages. The prize was 20,000 Pounds, an immense reward at the time. The story of the prize and the inventor, John Harrison, who eventually claimed it, is told in the 1995 book *Longitude* by Dava Sobel.

Chapter 14

1 Woolf, Steven H., Executive Vice President for Policy Development, Partnership for Prevention, and Professor of Family Medicine, Preventive Medicine and Community Health, Virginia Commonwealth University. Testimony before the Subcommittee on Health, Sept. 21, 2004, U.S. House of Representatives. Partnership for Prevention is a nonprofit, membership-based health policy organization based in Washington, DC. It advises decision makers in the public, private, and nonprofit sectors on policies and practices to prevent disease and injury and to promote health. Testimony available at http://www.prevent.org/pressRelease.cfm?id=16.

INDEX

ABOUT THE AUTHOR

Henry A. McKinnell joined Pfizer, Tokyo, in 1971 and since then has assumed positions of increasing responsibility at Pfizer operations around the world. Chairman since May 2001, McKinnell has enjoyed an illustrious career at the firm spanning more than 34 years and has received accolades for both his leadership ability and business acumen. In 2003, McKinnell was honored with the United Nations Association of America's Global Leadership Award and, in 2004, he was counted among America's most powerful business leaders by *Fortune* magazine.